HEALING

JULES

A Spiritual Journey to Heal People Pleasing,
Anxiety, and Codependency to Fall in Love
with Life Again.

JULIE CLAPP
SPIRITUAL MEDIUM, RN, BSN

ISBN: : 9798864555903

Chapter 1

The Book of Jewels

I have a vivid memory of being in sixth grade, early morning standing outside of my locker and having the completely overwhelming urge to puke, and then I did. So in shear embarrassment a teacher walks me to the nurses office to call my mom. This wasn't the first time I'd felt this, and it certainly wouldn't be the last. The funny part was, after I got home I felt fine. But nonetheless, many mornings following I felt the same. I wanted to stay home from school more and more. So, my mom eventually took me to the doctor. I don't remember much of what they did, but I do remember them telling me nothing was "wrong" with me and that it was more than likely just a "nervous belly." "Hmm, ok, just a nervous belly," I thought to myself. At that moment I developed a belief that this was just me, just my belly, and something I would have to embrace and tolerate in my life, and I did just that. As the years ensued, I fought through that familiar feeling many times, almost allowing myself to befriend it. I started to correlate it with big things that I was supposed to "push through." I also realized, the more I didn't let it win, the more accomplished I felt. Before long, an overachiever was born within me from that very belief, but over time that overachiever became exhausted and depleted.

I remember being 16 and sitting in Spanish class. The French teacher next door walked in and said, "I have a friend who is a doctor and is looking for some after school help with filing and office duties, anyone interested in a part time job?" Immediately I raised my hand. That next week I was in that office and so was my nervous belly friend. So of course, I told myself, this must be big, and it must be the right place for me. My Dad would pick me up after school each day and drop me off at work and then pick me up at 5:30pm when the office would close. These people became like a second family to me and offered me a full-time gig over the summer. The more time I spent there the more I felt at home. But the thing about my nervous belly was, if I felt it go away, I told myself I wasn't doing anything big, I wasn't going to accomplish anything, and so I would set out to push myself more, until I felt it again. It's almost as if I became addicted to that feeling, telling myself it was a good thing for me, even though it didn't feel that way. As I contemplated what was next for me, I realized I would need a car.

So, my sister and brother-in-law loaned me the money to get my first car- a purple Hyundai Excel. I loved it, I felt cool in it, but the only problem was it was a stick shift, and I had no idea how to drive it. My brother would take me on short trips in his car to try to teach me, but I wasn't quite getting it. I started to think, how am I going to drive to school without stalling and being the laughing stock? I asked my friends that knew how to drive it to come with me and drive in and out of the parking lot until I got the hang of it. Now that I had a car, I was ready to consider what I wanted to do.

I continued to work at the doctor's office throughout my senior year. I had fully planned to go to college to be a marine biologist. I'm a Scorpio, a water sign. I love the water even though, ironically, I was born with a deep fear of it. A fear that eventually once I conquered it, turned into a beautiful love story. One day my high school was offering a seminar and they were having a marine biologist from Wood's Hole Oceanographic Institute come and speak. I thought, "perfect!". As I'm sitting in the conference room, the speaker introduces himself and says right off the bat, "If you've come here because you want to explore a career in marine biology and you think you will be swimming with the dolphins in Hawaii or Australia, I'm going to tell you that's not the case." I can't remember my exact thought at that point, but I'm pretty sure it was something like, "shit, that's exactly how I envisioned it." He went on to say, "That's not what it's like. It's grueling days and nights in cold and wet New England weather with stinky fish. It's weeks out at sea away from your family getting seasick." My whole life plan was shot down in those five minutes. Immediately I go to my guidance counselor to discuss plan B.

Because I worked at a doctor's office and enjoyed it, he suggested considering a career in healthcare. Since I had so many nieces and nephews, I thought it would be great working with kids. I thought maybe a pediatrician. As I discussed that commitment with my guidance counselor it didn't sound as appealing. He suggested nursing where it is less of a school commitment with many avenues I could explore. Done. I applied to Boston University, Boston College, and Northeastern University. I got into all three, but Boston College was my top pick. It was also my Dad's favorite. I think he secretly always wanted an Eagle in his family. I'm not gonna lie, the financial load of that decision scared me. My parents had raised nine kids. They didn't have one hundred thousand dollars to spare for my college education and I didn't expect them to. I ended up picking

Northeastern because they gave me the best financial aid offer; nearly a free ride for my first year if I didn't live there. I decided to commute to cut costs.

Every morning I'd wake up at 5am, slap on a hat, get in my Hyundai and drive an hour and a half through grueling traffic into Boston. Some mornings my nervous belly would wake me up. My stomach was so sensitive I could throw up just brushing my teeth, but I'd just push through to get to school. It became my way of life. By the time I had gotten to my senior year, I was broke, and my car was so worn from commuting, it wouldn't even go in reverse. I'd make sure I'd pull into the local Dunkies and park on a hill so I could roll out backwards and be on my way. I remember scrounging up coins to pay for my morning coffee. Some mornings waking my mom up at 5am asking for five dollars to put gas in my car to get me to and from school. Yes, in 1996 five dollars went a long way for gas! Let me tell you these were some of the most character building and humbling days of my life. I was resolute to work hard and achieve my goals. The doctor's office I worked at helped me get a job as a certified nursing assistant at a local hospital. At that time nursing was a competitive field and there were not that many jobs for new graduates with no experience. I started working the 3-11 shift after school and weekends. Cue the nervous belly.

I was shell shocked once I got into the hospital environment. It wasn't really anything like I thought it was. It was a fast paced, high stress environment and I had no idea what I was doing. The energy in healthcare was hard for me to feel comfortable in. Again, my nervous belly and I pushed through because, after all, we were doing great things, or so I told myself to persevere. My first day I was thankfully working with another student nurse from school. One of the Registered Nurses pulled me aside and said, "Muriel in 273 is done on the bedpan, you're gonna need towels, facecloths and probably a nose clip." My face dropped. My first code brown. I remember this woman as a doppelgänger to Mama Fratelli, the "Ma" of the two criminals in the movie Goonies. She even sounded like her. The fear welled up inside me and I was too scared to ask her to help or show me what to do. I begged my nursing friend to come with me. I grabbed everything but the nose clip, apparently that was a joke, and they don't really have those in healthcare. "I would have to purchase my own," I thought. In that moment I realized I had a lot more control over my stomach than I had given myself credit for. A new resilience was born within me.

My nursing career was pretty much the same. I started out terrified and feeling unqualified but somehow, I ended up graduating Cum Laude with my BSN. But just because Northeastern University and the Massachusetts State Boards said I was ready, my mind and my stomach didn't agree. These were real people, and I was responsible for their well-being. Thankfully all of the people I worked with were amazing. After all, we were in the trenches together, we were a team and became a dysfunctional family of our own with a loyalty so deep it was palpable. To this day, some of these people are still my best friends and I would be there ride or die in a heartbeat if they needed me. I remember my first code experience, not code brown, code blue. I was in shear panic. I remember my hands shaking and my voice quivering when the doctor asked me about my patient. I also remember looking at the nurses that rushed in on the code team and how they were saving a life like it was their second nature. As my Dad would always say, "No big deal." I was in awe of them. How did they do it so fearlessly and confidently? A loud voice inside me said, "I want to be them."

So down the road towards all my fears I went, and you guessed it, my nervous belly rode shot gun the whole way. Indeed, we were doing great things again. I started to show up for work nearly an hour early so I could get my assignment and have time to research my patients to make me feel more comfortable. Early on in my nursing career I was thrust into a leadership role because it looked like I took initiative to be in charge and I was conscientious. What they didn't see is I was really just scared shitless, and trying to have some control over my environment made me feel better and more prepared. It silenced the bells and whistles of my nervous system enough to perform. Over the years I did everything I was afraid of. I got certified in telemetry, in peritoneal dialysis, I did pediatrics, and eventually took a management position that pushed me into every code, rapid response and emergency situation that arose. Eventually I became that nurse by the bedside on the code team. I strived to make the new grad who was trembling in the corner like I used to feel safe and like somebody had their back. All of these achievements continued to fuel my drive to achieve, my perfectionism, my need for control, and the belief that anxiety was my friend.

Fast forward fifteen years. If you read my first book, "Waking Jules" you know that in my mid-thirties is when my spiritual awakening started. Looking back, I remember finding out that my Dad was diagnosed with ALS a few months prior. I'll never forget that day he came to talk to me. I burst into tears, and he took his big pointer finger and tapped the side of my cheek. He said, "I don't ever want to see you do that again. You're gonna be fine. We can do this." Indeed, we did. I remember shortly after having what I now recognize was a panic attack. I realized that I had them a few times before in my younger years, I just never knew what they were. I explained them away as "I must need to eat something," or "maybe I'm coming down with something." This time, I knew. It was the first time I said to myself, "I have anxiety" and it didn't resonate with being a good thing anymore. I went to my doctor, and she prescribed Citalopram 10mg. She also gave me a prescription for Xanax 0.5mg in case I needed it during a panic attack. I took the Xanax once and I never took it again. It did get rid of my anxiety, but it made me feel completely numb. As a sensitive and empath, numbness was scarier than anxiety for me. When it wore off, all of my feelings rushed back in like a wave for me to then process after the fact. I knew it did not serve me. I continued on the Citalopram which felt like a miracle to me. Even when I was doing something great, or when I was doing something I was afraid of, my nervous belly didn't seem to show up as much. I also recognized that the intermittent tightness in my chest I would feel when stressed wasn't as predominant. What I had labeled as "just who I am" and what I had to learn to live with for so many years was anxiety.

I wondered if I had been told that all of those years ago and offered help, would the course of those years had been different for me? Nonetheless, I was where I was, and I looked at it as an opportunity to change it now. I stayed on the Citalopram for years. After my Dad died and I allowed myself to process my grief, I told my doctor that I wanted to try to come off of it. I was a different person at that point. I gave my notice at my nursing job three months before my Dad passed. At that time, my medium business was doing good enough that I knew it could supplement enough income for me to stay home, help my Dad and I could do nursing per diem, on the side. As a medium I had daily practices of meditation, etc. that greatly improved my thoughts and feelings which helped my anxiety, but never fully relieved it. Over the following years I was able to come off of the medicine for periods of time and I would go back on if I was going through a stressful event that triggered panic attacks. If you've never had a panic attack, I would describe it as a hot flash that surges through your body and makes you feel like you are going to throw up, pass out, or both. It is a scary feeling to feel out of control of your own body. The medicine gave me some of that power back without numbing me. Nonetheless, years later when the pandemic hit, my panic attacks resurfaced. Everything felt out of control, uncertain, and stressful. My high risk 80-year-old mom lived with me that I was trying to keep safe. I wouldn't even let her leave the house to do her own food shopping. I became the designated shopper. I felt like my nursing background prepared me in some ways, but not enough. I decided to convert my two boys to remote learning, which was basically like homeschool so that it would lessen the chances of covid reaching my mom. In addition, my medium business, which was booked a year out, was wiped clean. I had to start from scratch and learn how to recreate my business virtually if I wanted to survive and have an income. The thing about being self-employed is if you don't work, you don't get paid. I knew this level of stress and anxiety coursing through my body was at a level I had never felt before. I could also feel it with others I would encounter. The energy of fear was palpable, and it put a lot of strain on the relationships in my life. It was at this point I remember saying to God, "please help me to heal my anxiety." If a soul could feel tired, mine was. I sat in the bathroom with the door closed, where no one would hear me or see tears rolling down my face and I whispered, "Jesus, I'm tired of suffering. Please help me and I promise I will share everything I learn along the way." Just a few months later, I started writing this book.

REFLECTIONS & NOTES CHAPTER 1

Chapter 2

"You Cannot Solve a Problem with the Same Mind that Created it" ~ Einstein

Wayne Dyer said, "when we change the way we look at things, the things we look at change." Wayne was introduced to me by my sister. I loved his work and I leaned into it as part of my healing. Essentially, I came to the realization that how we feel is never really about the conditions on the outside. It's all about what the conditions on the inside are, the inner climate, and my inner climate felt chaotic and stormy. When you feel broken and lost and disempowered that is not only the way you will experience the world you live in, that is also the launching point of creation of your new experiences.

The Law of Attraction states that the energy level we vibrate at in each moment is our point of attraction. Like a magnet, what we think and feel is a reflection of the energy we embody, and that is what we bring about. Much of those thoughts and feelings are really meant to just provide us awareness of that energy and to be the catalyst that can lead us to higher ground, and greater potential within ourselves. What if these storms were really just doorways to our consciousness, and our innate wisdom as a soul having a human experience? Remember when Mother Theresa said, "It was never really between you and them anyways; it was always between you and God."? I believe this is what she meant. Our experiences are mirrors that are constantly reflecting something within us- perhaps a part of ourselves that is undiscovered, unrecognized, unloved, unhealed, or undervalued.

So, if you are still here with me, we are going on a healing journey together to discover all of this. I will share my journey with you in hopes that there will be parts that serve as a mirror for you, to discover your "un's" and transform them into "able's". We are going to take grand bold leaps to what is on the inside. What is within that is calling to be healed. What is within that is tired and begging to be released. What is within that may have been holding us back from "feeling good" or keeping us from more blissful moments. It doesn't matter if what led you here is not feeling good mentally, or not feeling good emotionally, or not feeling good physically! We are going to uncover the layers of the "not feeling good." We are going to acknowledge the root cause and we are going to take the third step toward lovingly healing and releasing it, instead of beating ourselves up about it! You know you are never really giving yourself the credit you deserve, don't you? I bet you didn't know that you are already on step 3 of your healing journey. You've already done the first two steps. Step 1 was the day you acknowledged that some experiences or conditions in your life have taken over your inner climate. Step 2 was the day you listened to the still small voice of your soul within that knows things can be different and you deserve that. That voice led you here to this book right now. My hope is that this book shows you just how powerful you really are.

REFLECTIONS & NOTES CHAPTER 2

Chapter 3

"Is it Worth it? Let me work It. I put my thang down. Flip it and reverse it." ~Missy Elliott

Just like a weed in a garden, pain must be released by the root, or it just regenerates growth each time it is given light. Without tending to that garden within those weeds will eventually stifle your growth and keep you stuck in patterns. This healing journey will help us to see more clearly the subconscious and conscious patterns we develop that fuel our unwellness more than our wellness. It will also help to clearly see the distinction of the conditioned mind and the intuitive mind. One is always in the driver's seat, and to be in your power is to always be aware of who's in charge.

My hope is that while reading these pages you will witness the beautiful and synchronistic relationship between your mental body, emotional body and physical body and you will begin to acknowledge how they are constantly conspiring with one another for our highest good. Part of the healing journey is to acknowledge our wounds for the truth of what they really are. They are the portals to our consciousness, our wisdom, and they can serve as the catalyst to break cycles. Cycles and patterns deeply engrained in our subconscious, within our family units, and within our ancestral soul circles. So, whether or not you realize it, your healing journey is not only to serve you, it is to serve your ancestors, your family now, future generations and humanity as a whole. You are about to uncover, discover, and come home to more of the true and simply beautiful authenticity of your soul so that you can freely and fearlessly express it out into this world as you knew you would. I pray that as you read these pages, they will empower you to allow all those beautiful gifts God placed within you to rise like a phoenix from the ashes of your pain, to reignite the fire of your soul, and to light up this world. I want you to create a beautiful new chapter in your story that goes something like this, "The day I fell in love with life again..."

JULIE CLAPP

REFLECTIONS & NOTES CHAPTER 3

Chapter 4

"But there's a hope that's waiting for you in the dark, you should know that you're beautiful just the way you are," ~Alessia Cara

When I first started my mediumship journey 10 years ago, spirit gave me a clear message that I didn't quite have a full understanding of at the time. They said, "to Know thyself is to understand others." Looking back, I now know what they meant. They were letting me know that this journey of mediumship was part of my soul contract. My mediumship was a journey of self-discovery. The more I learned about myself, the more I began to understand others. The more I tapped into the compassion and grace within me, the more I was able to extend that compassion and grace to others. Now this didn't mean that I'm always in that space of compassion and grace. The irony is that I had to be willing to go into the deepest darkest corners of my own shadows and heal them in order to access that compassion and grace on a new level. Getting a taste of what it felt like to travel from a depth within yourself to a new height of emotion and vibration was pivotal for me. I had to learn to embrace my discomfort and feel all things. This was the birthplace of that initial awareness of a power within me to feel so much better.

Once you know this power, you can't unknow it. This brings us to crave that new energy level more and more and to discover the tools within us to achieve it. We no longer settle for the darkness. We continually seek the light because we know it's always there. For some in the spiritual community this epiphany and craving can lead to spiritual bypassing and toxic positivity. I can definitely see where I began to practice that on my journey in an attempt to alleviate my discomfort without having to go deep and feel it. It's the premise, if I have the power to always feel better, than why would I need to feel anything else, right? Wrong. Within a few short years I noticed that in spiritually bypassing my emotional guidance system when I felt dense emotion, I was not only undermining my intuition, I was also dysregulating my nervous system. Nonetheless, it was a layer of consciousness that I needed to access before I would take those deep dives and begin to heal. It was that very power that would help me rise over and over again.

The reason I say again, is that I've learned our journeys are not linear as we perceive them and correlate them to time.

My therapist who I will introduce you to later always said to me, "healing is not a destination." Our journeys are cyclical. Healing and manifesting happen in cycles where with each rotation we access new levels of our consciousness, and from my experience, new freedom and bliss. In order for the cycle to happen, the deep dives are necessary. So, in essence our vibration is not meant to be "high" all the time. It is meant to ebb and flow. Those shifts don't happen in heaven, only here, what if that's what we really came for?

I learned a lot in those early years of my mediumship about myself and about others. I talked a lot in "Waking Jules" that much of my journey of awakening my intuitive and mediumistic abilities was about bringing myself to new levels of compassion, grace, empathy and understanding. It's the natural vibration of our soul. Our souls crave it because before we chose to enter this world, it's what we knew. It's a constant frequency of energy in that dimension we call "heaven." What I realized as I embarked on my healing journey, was that nursing and mediumship always had me focusing and directing that compassion, empathy and understanding outward to others. It wasn't until my inner climate was out of control and so dysregulated that I realized I needed to give some of it to myself.

When we choose to enter this physical body, we sign up to feel contrasting emotions that we do not feel in heaven. In heaven exists a steady stream of consciousness that vibrates at an energy level of pure and unconditional love. Unconditional love, i.e., a love that is a constant and does not waver and is not "dependent upon any conditions." That is what our soul knows to be true and what it is used to feeling. Then we- as pure souls filled with light- decide to come into this world within this dense body. This dense body has a brain and a nervous system, with needs and wants, with thoughts, feelings and emotions that at times all seem to be working against us. But the truth is, they are not. They are guiding us! They are the still small voice within that is always looking out for us, when we allow it to be.

Most of the emotions that we view as negative or low vibrations are dense. They are pain, sadness, anger, grief, jealousy, fear, worry, frustration, lack, less than, insecurity, guilt, shame, disappointment, blame, doubt, impatience, and the list goes on and on. When we focus on them for too long, we give them momentum and we expand them which can eventually cause them to manifest as physical illness in the body.

Pat Longo, my dearest mentor and spiritual healer friend describes "dis-ease" as just anything that blocks the natural flow of our energy and our life force. Essentially if we do not pay attention to where we are focusing our energy, we will inevitably fall ill in some form. Mental and emotional unwellness will always over time and without tending, manifest physically in the body. In addition, physical illness over time and without tending will manifest mentally and emotionally in the body. Therefore, dense emotions require tending. They weigh us down and pull us further and further away from that truth of our soul. This is why awareness and knowing how to feel better is just as important as knowing you need to allow yourself to feel those emotions to heal. It is the still small voice of our soul that reminds us, "hey you, don't forget, this feeling is just temporary, it isn't who you are."

That's the thing, we often start to define ourselves by our emotions. When we feel a certain emotion long enough, we start to develop beliefs about ourselves in response to them. We develop patterns of behavior that don't serve us in order to alleviate them. Dr. Joe Dispenza says a thought we keep thinking will trigger an emotion on replay. An emotion on replay will eventually turn into a mood, and a mood that lasts too long will eventually become a personality trait. Hence, allowing our emotions to define who we are. Who we really are is "unconditional love." So, our emotional guidance system is always attempting to guide us back to that truth when we are pulled away from it by conditions. Sometimes that journey back to that truth can be a long and tenuous one. Sometimes it can be instantaneous. Why? Because we have a scale of emotional responses. Depending on where we fall in that emotional scale, determines how deep the wound is. Rumi says, "the wound is the place where the light enters."

Deeper wounds, like trauma wounds, will require more healing and tending. Lighter wounds can be healed and released sometimes instantaneously. What makes all the difference is your launching point of energy. For example, have you ever had a day where you completely amazed yourself? Meaning you just felt so on your game, and nothing could threaten your vibe? Where everything that could go wrong did, like your car breaking down, a call with bad news, a person in line being rude to you, and yet, you remained unscathed and untouchable? You know- an Alicia keys, "this girl is on fire" kind of day? Alternately have you ever had a day where simply spilling your morning cup of coffee feels like the end of the world and life itself? A day where you are ready to just hang up your wings because that one moment was the final straw that broke your little angel's back? The only difference between those scenarios was your vibrational launching pad, or starting point. What was true for me in my experience was the more I bypassed and tried avoiding doing the healing work, the less capacity I had to deal with challenges and stressors in my life. Over time my fuse got shorter and shorter because my nervous system was becoming more dysregulated. It was begging me to do the work and so I did.

JULIE CLAPP

REFLECTIONS & NOTES CHAPTER 4

Chapter 5

"Don't Judge each day by the harvest you reap, but by the seed you plant." ~Robert Louis Stevenson

If you were a garden that had the ability to grow beautiful and nurturing food and flowers, what would happen as weeds begin to pop up? We know as the sun brings more light and growth, inevitably, weeds too will grow. For the sake of this argument let's view the weeds as the people, circumstances, or conditions that injure us, stifle us, or create wounds within us. The more weeds you let grow in your garden, the more wounds you are leaving untended. Undoubtedly over time this will leave you in a vibration of defeat, of despair, and of complete disempowerment. Unable to see the light or catch your breath, you will live your life moment to moment with a feeling of impending doom, with a black cloud following you around, and you will be in a deep state of suffering, suffocated by the weeds in your garden. Sound familiar? This is the great illusion of the ego, or the wounded child within you that is looking to be saved.

The truth is, you are the garden, you are the flowers, and you are the gardener. God made you that way. Tending your garden and healing the wounds will never come at the hands of anyone or anything outside of you, it comes from within you! The most incredible silver lining that is offered to you within the darkness, is, that in life, the depth at which you feel or experience your darkness is directly proportionate to the height with which you experience your light! So that depth of darkness offers you an opportunity, with tending and healing, to rise into a higher vibration and consciousness than you've ever known before! As you learn to alchemize, or transform your feelings, you call more light into your energy body. You "embody" more love through self-love and by acknowledging those shadow parts. Those are the parts of yourself deeply hidden below the surface of your conditioning and patterns of behavior you developed to soothe the ego. The parts of you that didn't receive the energy, compassion, love or attention it needed at a certain time. As a result of doing the healing work and tending, you access that consciousness of your soul that exists at a higher frequency of energy. It becomes the dominant energy of your energy body. You become more "in tune" with your intuition and your abilities to create a whole new experience of your life become possible.

The thing about us humans is that we are always looking to avoid those uncomfortable feelings, but what would happen if we allowed ourselves to feel into them fully? When we silence our feelings, we silence our intuition, our inner guidance system. Our nervous system is a built-in navigation system that is meant to guide us to what is in our highest and best good in any given moment. In discomfort, we often crave the quick fix to alleviate the pain instead of allowing ourselves to feel the pain. Our past experiences condition the subconscious mind to fear feeling pain, all the while our soul is cueing our nervous system to scream at us to look deeper into the pain to get to the root of it.

The quick fix provides temporary relief and hence, patterns of behavior are born that only perpetuate the growth of our weeds, and keep us stuck in cycles that repeat. Those quick fixes can range from addictions to drugs, alcohol, food, and sex, to addictive patterns of behavior, such as manipulation and control. Those pesky little weeds that take your pain and take root in your ego, create the story line of, "I'll protect you, you can't possibly handle this!" All the while your little pure soul knows that not only can you handle it, but you can also heal it, so it tries to tell you a different story. Not just a different script;

it's a different genre all together. A tug of war between the protector mind, or the ego, and your spirit ensues. Your soul stands tall in your abilities and it says, "remember who you are and what you are capable of."

You are a child of God with the purest stream of love, grace, strength, and resiliency flowing through to you at all times. You are a miracle. You have the ability to create miracles and you have the ability to build walls against them. In your greatest moments of discomfort your soul is asking you, "are you building your miracle, or are you building a wall right now?" You can't be giving your attention or focus to both at the same time. That is your power. To use your free will to choose. To choose to focus and give energy to the solution or the problem, to the wellness, or to the unwellness, to the disease or to the cure, to the pain or to the healing. I hope by now that the volume of your still small voice has temporarily drowned out the noise of your pain and has you up out of your seat jumping and screaming, yes, yes! I am ready to feel better, I am ready for more, I am ready to feel all my feels, I am ready to tend to my garden, I am ready to breathe again. I am ready to feel the joy of creating my miracles, and I am ready to break down those old walls that have been blocking me!

REFLECTIONS & NOTES CHAPTER 5

Chapter 6

It's Trauma not Drama

My definition of trauma is any individualized painful experience. Trauma has varying degrees and scales, none of which can be compared and that is why it is individualized. You could take two different people and have them undergo the same surgery and they would recover differently. The variable factors in that scenario have to do with their perspective launching points prior to the surgery, i.e, what was their state of wellness prior to it and their history? In addition, there are the uncontrollable variables, which are everything and everyone else, including but not limited to the environment, the caregivers, the support, the availability, the timing, etc. All of these factors will contribute to our responses to our life experiences and our recovery from them. All of these factors also play a role in our recovery of trauma, even emotional trauma.

We all have trauma. Some may not label it that because they have spent years comparing their painful experiences to the experiences of others. I did that for years. I truly believed I had no trauma. They may not label it trauma because they think in some way, they would sound overly dramatic and would be risking their vulnerability. Some may not call it trauma because it "feels better" to call it something else. Some may not call it trauma because they have been conditioned not to, somebody always has it worse right? Not necessarily, and there is no need to diminish whatever your trauma has been to you. Whatever your reasons, the experiences are yours and they are not up for judgement, but the truth is, everyone has trauma. The degree of trauma solely depends on you and how deeply rooted the wound is. Mastin Kipp says, "unhealed trauma will block manifestation." This means that over time, those walls pinch us off from that truth of our soul. The voice of our pain is the loudest voice we hear. We cut ourselves off from our power to create, to build, and to manifest our heart's desires; we suffocate our bliss. This is why it is so important to recognize when we have trauma that is calling to be healed. You may be asking, how does trauma called to be healed? Well, mine was calling to be healed through my triggers.

Triggers are the nervous system's response when a wound is accessed. When someone pokes that wound whether intentionally or unintentionally it causes a rush of emotion to flood back in. That rush, no matter how much time has passed, can bring you right back to the point of pain or traumatic experiences. In Dr. Bessel Van Der Kolk's, "The Body Keeps the Score" he talks about many psychological studies that were done on veterans surrounding their traumatic experiences. The discoveries were basically that no matter how much time passes after a traumatic event, the brain and the cells of the body have memory recall, and can reproduce the same effect repeatedly. Even with lesser stimuli, that memory will be triggered. So, something that would seemingly be "less catastrophic" than the original event, can still trigger the same emotional and physical response from the nervous system, even many years later. What many people, including myself, didn't realize is that symptoms of PTSD (Post Traumatic Stress Disorder) and CPTSD (Complex Post Traumatic Stress Disorder, which is only recently recognized in the DSM-5 under Trauma and Stressor related disorders) , does not have a prerequisite of being a war veteran to take root in the nervous system. Many of us have fought silent wars that we've diminished for years, and our nervous systems are now asking to be heard.

After my Dad died nine years ago, I remember telling everyone around me how broken I was for a long time. I made sure everyone knew the extent of my pain. I felt if I kept telling everyone how broken I was, maybe they wouldn't expect anything of me, and I wouldn't feel bad about not being able to meet any of their needs. The first part of this, is that the pain and trauma of losing my Dad brought me to a new level of dense emotion than I had ever felt, hence, the deep wound. Second, other people triggering me every time they asked me for something, and I projected it onto them as being "needy" was just a deflection. It was me using my pain to deflect the real root of the problem which I did not realize at the time. At its core I was hurt and grieving. Abraham Hicks says, "grieving and sadness are two of the lowest emotions we can feel on the vibrational scale." At this level our ego will kick into high gear and tell us stories of how we need to protect ourselves and who from. After all, we cannot possibly endure any more pain. I felt if I just kept reminding everyone around me that I was already so hurt, maybe, they just would not do or say anything that would make me feel uncomfortable or hurt more. This is a trauma response.

Pain and trauma can make us feel out of control, so the ego, or logical mind, seeks protection by attempting to control situations and the people around us. We become hypervigilant at seeking out our perceived threats and instinctually push them away. For a while this may work, but eventually the truth comes to light. Eventually those around you will grow tired of walking on eggshells and not having a reciprocal relationship and balanced energetic exchange. I'm sure you can think of times where you've felt like people in your life had you walking on eggshells or never reciprocated the energy you gave to the relationship and got fed up. Eventually people start honoring and making decisions that are in their best interests, not out of pleasing others. What and who we can no longer control will eventually become a perceived threat to the ego. When we are only able to see through the peep hole of our pain, our lens of acceptance is very narrow. So, we push anyone and anything away that is a perceived threat. Eventually, those feelings of being alone, unsupported, and isolated become a self-fulfilling prophecy. Your external world becomes a reflection of your internal condition. This is true for so many because there is a lack of awareness of the wound, the ego's role, and our power in healing it.

My husband was undoubtedly the one that led me to my healing. Not because he "loved me more" as my ego was seeking, but because he constantly challenged me in a loving way to see things differently. He became a mirror for me to see me. That resistance from the people closest to me is what led me to self-reflect. Resistance leads to reflection. Resistance is uncomfortable and when there are fewer people to deflect and blame it on, we are left looking at the person in the mirror. When people stop doing the dance with you, and you find yourself dancing alone, you eventually will learn to sit still with yourself. My process of reflection was a process that I did over and over again, until I was able to separate my pain from my overall perception of life. I was able to say, yes, I am grieving, but that does not mean a life of stress, heartache, and resistance. Or yes, I am feeling this in response to that right now, but this too shall pass.

The more I peeled back the layers in my self-reflection the more I uncovered other weeds. Traumas that I didn't recognize as trauma before, showed up to reveal themselves to me. The triggers and the resistance were showing me exactly what needed to be healed layer by layer. One by one I acknowledged them. I acknowledged them and I felt them. I peeled back the layers of them until I got to the exact moment that each wound was born. When we get to the birthplace of the wound, we can console the ego or the inner child that is trying to protect itself. We can make our wounded child feel safe again. Give him/her love and acceptance and compassion that is needed. Then we can clearly see the patterns we need to release that no longer protect us.

While allowing my feelings without fear of them, I allowed more stuff to lovingly rise to the surface. I had known for years that I was a people pleaser at my core, and I honestly prided myself on it. I thought that pleasing people is a good thing, right? Actually no, people pleasing is just a layer to a self-worth wound. It is an unconscious manipulation to control others' perceptions of us, so that we always feel loved and worthy of love. That is why the thought of not being able to meet others needs when I was grieving, was paralyzing to me. I worked diligently on changing this pattern, but it was always very challenging for me. People pleasers tend to feel good when they are pleasing others. Alternately they tend to feel really bad when they are not pleasing others. A belief is then born that we must "please" to feel good.

At first, I didn't really know where this belief was born from within me, but I knew it was a pattern for a long period of time. In the midst of my healing work, one morning I woke up to a semi-conscious daydream. It brought me back to when I was a young girl. I was shy and introverted. In school I would play by myself, and my teachers would tell my mom that they were concerned by my social isolation. I wonder how they would feel now? I can seemingly imagine that I was probably not really isolated at all, just connecting more to those that others couldn't see. Wink. Instinctively, even at a young age, I kept my circle very small and didn't overtly trust easily. In my daydream, I remembered that I had a friend that I trusted who convinced me to do something that I knew was wrong. In case you're wondering, sweet little Julie stole something from the local Brooks pharmacy. I felt it in my gut. But because I trusted her, and I wanted to be liked by her, I abandoned my higher guidance and did it anyway. I remember the overwhelming feeling of shame and guilt.

My mom used to play a game with me where she would always have me calculate the change at the drive-through's like McDonald's and Wendy's. If the worker was even a penny off, my mom always made it a point to let them know and correct it, even when it would've worked in our favor. She would always remind me, if we didn't do that, it would come out of their own paycheck at the end of the night. So now you can understand why stealing made me feel so ashamed. Well, that's not necessarily a bad thing, right? It teaches us to not do those things again. It teaches us right and wrong. Do you know what it taught me? It taught me that I never wanted to feel what it felt like for others to be disappointed in me again, and so my journey as a people pleaser was born.

At the core, people pleasing is a means to control and manipulate how others feel about you. It is the greatest disconnection from self. It is a belief that the only way to receive unconditional love and avoidance of rejection is to become a shapeshifter of whatever is needed in the moment. I would do whatever it took to avoid that feeling of shame or disappointment, even if it meant abandoning my higher guidance system. After all, I had done that before. Even though it didn't work out in my favor, it became an unconscious, but necessary evil of avoiding disappointment, shame, and guilt and receiving love. Over time this belief can become our tool to measure our worth and esteem. In other words, the happier people are with us, the better we feel about ourselves. People pleasing becomes a subconscious pattern of manipulation to receive more love and praise when we feel depleted of it. We are saying yes when we actually want to say no, essentially setting the people in our lives up to be resented. The underlying notion of the ego or wounded child is- because I'm overextending myself, you will love me more. Over time the word "No" becomes taboo because we equate it to feelings of shame, guilt, and inadequacy. So, we say yes and we please and please, seeking extrinsic sources to fill up our depleted tanks. Once in a state of depletion, if you are asked for something you will have to find a character defect or reason to place blame on the person asking. Why? Because you know you don't have anything left to give! Your tank is empty and everyone else is to blame. It is easier to place blame than to deal with the shame of having to say no.

Ahhh the ego has now learned to project this wound on another, so it doesn't have to face what is at the core. At this point, if you continue to say yes from places of depletion you breed cycles of resentment in relationships. Now that is not to say that you are not aligning yourself with "takers." You more than likely are, because you are emitting a "giving" energy. What if those "takers" were just the mirror you needed to acknowledge the wound? Resentments eventually lead to distance and separation. The truth of what is really going on, is that your inner child is screaming, "why can't they see I'm in pain?" The truth is your soul is whispering, "this has nothing to do with them, it has everything to do with you." You are the healer of you. Others are just leading you to it.

Once you can step back from that peep hole lens of your pain to get a broader view, you can see things differently and more clearly without the resentment for who people are. You begin to realize that feelings are temporary. You begin to realize that there is no amount of love on the outside that will ever be enough when what is on the inside is running low. You begin to realize that "No" is not selfish it is often necessary for self-preservation and the hallmark of the healthy sense of self. If you remove the word no from your vocabulary, thinking it is selfish, you will undoubtedly suffer self-abandonment wounds from repeatedly doing what is best for everyone else rather than what your higher self is saying is best for you. Eventually, you lose your sense of self. If you haven't noticed from this downward spiral I have just described, trauma will completely disempower you, negatively impact your relationships and it will steal your joy as long as you allow it too. But if you use this knowledge to your advantage, you can transform your trauma into your greatest comeback. You can use your trauma to discover a new level of empowerment. You can use it to build stronger, healthier, more respectful and authentic relationships in your life. You can use it to bring more joy into your life than you ever allowed before because you made room for it. Releasing all the pain and getting to the bliss of your healing and "aha moments, creates space for joy, so much space for so much more joy! To transform your trauma, you have to be willing to step back from that peep hole and take a good long look at who is in the mirror. You have to get comfortable with some level of discomfort. You have to discover the patterns of how your ego is responding to your triggers that are culminating the problem instead of the remedy. I realized that in my grief my attempt to control and manipulate others into pleasing me, was a direct reflection of my own issue with people pleasing. Why don't people love me the way I love them? Why won't people sacrifice themselves for me like I will for them? Why won't people abandon their higher guidance system to do what I want them to do to make me happy, when I am willing to do that for them? Do you see the patterns of how our wounded child serves to protect ourselves from obtaining more wounds? The answer to my inner child's questions was, "not everyone is a people pleaser, not everyone is you". Some people know how to self-preserve and are comfortable with setting boundaries to do so. Awakened sensitives, healers, empaths, intuitives, and psychic mediums, typically have a harder time with this. Does that speak to you? If so, let that sink in. As healers we feel everything on such a great level in order to do our work, so we do not want to feel any more discomfort than we have to. Ironically, it is within our work that we will be led to heal our own wounds. "The one who pulls out of the dark place becomes the medicine man, and the one who stays in it is the sick person." ~Joan Halifax

Once I acknowledged that in people pleasing, I was abandoning myself, and silencing the voice of my intuitive guidance, I was able to stop expecting others to do the same for me. I was projecting my own unhealthy patterns on the people around me. The first step to healing is awareness. Once I could see things differently, I could choose differently. I could stop saying yes when I didn't really want to. I could stop making choices that made others happy and me miserable and then blaming them for it. I could honor when others did not meet my expectations for what it truly was, them honoring their inner voice and guidance system; them following their own path of least resistance, them taking care of themselves. I started to realize, if others couldn't possibly know what was best for me in any given moment, how could I possibly know what was best for them?

And so, the stronghold of resistance and expectations was released, and acceptance was born anew. Healing takes time, and in the process, we will experience many triggers to get us to condition our responses in new ways. The resistance does not just melt away. This is a conditioning that was active in our vibration for many years. Therefore, it takes time to recondition. So, did I still attract people who I perceived as taking advantage of me? Yes. Did I now use them as an opportunity to change my response? Yes. The more we respond from this new place, this healed place, the lighter and freer we feel. We let go of the dense emotions of shame, guilt, resentment, blame, anger, and sadness. They are replaced with self-love, respect, acceptance, and joy. In removing the weed by the root, we clear the obstacle and restore our natural flow of wellbeing. You actually heal your vibration. You start to function at a higher frequency as you feel more sovereign to use your free will not to feed your ego and avoid discomfort. The truth is, you will lose some people as a result of this. Some people who were only attracted to the people pleaser in you, will leave. They will no longer align with your energy. The other truth is, you will start to notice the people that stay, or the people that come in closer, are the ones who always just loved you for you, not what you did for them. They will cheer you on and support you standing in your power. Ultimately, these too will be the sovereign folks in your life. They align with the energy of sovereignty. And so, you'll begin to see that God and the universe is truly always looking out for you, even when it does not appear that way; even when things seem hard. You are being led to more of the true and beautiful you! This is a great time to pause, reflect and do some journaling that will take you to the next steps of your healing journey. Use these prompts to help you get started and just let the feelings flow freely. No need to judge them, just honor them as they come up, and love them into the light.

- Did this help you to see more clearly some of your own triggers?
- What are they?
- What were they reflecting back to you?
- What wounds are calling to be healed?
- Can you peel back the layers of these multi-dimensional wounds to specific occurrences where they were born? Perhaps in childhood?
- What beliefs did you create about yourself as a result of those wounds?
- How has your inner wounded child prompted your ego to create patterns to protect yourself?
- What does your life look like not from the peep hole of your pain, but through the lens of your healed self?
- What can you release now, to make more room for joy?

- What can you do to you let more joy in everyday?

JULIE CLAPP

REFLECTIONS & NOTES CHAPTER 6

Chapter 7

"You can't focus on the wound and the healing at the same time."

Abraham Hicks say, "where attention goes, energy flows." Now even if you don't believe in the law of attraction, we can start with some concepts that have a little more solid scientific foundation for you to grasp. The Law of Conservation of Energy tells us that energy is neither created nor destroyed. It is simply transferred and transformed into various states. We are energetic beings. Even the energy and currents of our heartbeats can be measured. It is logical therefore to conclude that if we emit energy, based on the laws, not only can we transfer energy to one another, we are all powerful in manipulating and transforming our own energy states on multidimensional levels. Multidimensional in the physical world or dimension, and in the nonphysical, or spiritual dimension.

The reason this is relevant when it comes to our wounds and healing is because if we are giving all of our time, energy, and focus to our trauma and our wounds, then that is essentially what we are expanding. That is what we are putting out into the universe with our co-creative power. Essentially, we are shouting, "hey universe, I'd like more of this, please." See the universe, God or whatever label you prefer to give your creator for all intents and purposes, doesn't respond to what you say you want. The universe doesn't hear "I want this" and "I don't want that." It selectively just hears "this" and "that." You will receive both equally to the extent of your focus on them. The Universe gives you what you expect, not what you hope for or want. You get what is active and using energy within you. You can't fool the universe.

So, if you have felt like your life has been spent mostly in suffering, more than likely it is because you have been conditioned to expect it and, in some way, try to prepare for more of it. Of course, you do! If this is you, I want you to know that now is the time to be really gentle with yourself. It takes that one incident when trauma is born for you to be on your guard for the next time lightning will strike again. The survival part of the brain, the amygdala, can actually enlarge with trauma, and lead us to these very forms of hypervigilance and protective mechanisms. Staying on your toes becomes a pattern and a way of life where we think we are protecting or somehow preparing ourselves for the next blow. The truth is, we are being held captive by our fears and we are affirming to the universe that we are ready for it to serve up much more of the same. Hence the constant feelings of impending doom and the hovering dark clouds that follow.

Now my guess is your saying, but what about all those prayers I say every day, do they not work? Yes, they work. But if you spend 10 minutes a day in prayer, and then spend the other 23 hours and 50 minutes in fear, where do you think the majority of your power will go? Prayer is powerful. Do you know what makes it even more powerful? When you are using it to align with the energy of your creator. When you are using it as a tool to shift your energy level from fear up the vibrational scale to faith. You can say your prayers, and a million affirmations a day, but please allow them to empower you. God and the universe connect with you on an emotional level, not through your voice. Our energy is transferred through the power of our thoughts and emotions, what makes up our vibration or frequency, not just words. The most important prayer I say each day is, "Thy will be done through me." Essentially, I affirm to my creator, my God, I have utmost faith that as I align to his energy, I can do all things. I allow that wisdom, compassion, grace, and wellbeing to flow through me. I'm not asking God to do it for me, I'm asking God to help me to do things as he would do things. I surrender to the higher guidance and plan, knowing from my vantage point, I do not always know what is best. I trust and have faith that even when I can't see, my creator can. One of my favorite prayers of surrender to God's will I learned years ago is from Gabby Bernstein, and it is from "A Course In Miracles." It goes, "Where would you have me go today, what would you have me do, what would you have me say, and to whom?"

How does this lead to healing? If you are focused on the wound, you cannot be pouring as much energy into the healing. Now we just did all that work of going back to essentially reveal the sources of our trauma. In staying there, we will be stuck. We will simply be reliving the emotions attached to the wound. The purpose of going back is simply to reveal the information we need to move forward unobstructed. Once we see the role of our ego in our attempts to protect, we can identify our patterns of behavior that need changing. We can see more clearly the ways we have perpetuated our pain, instead of our healing. In the revelation of all of these things, we are afforded the opportunity to change them. In fact, each time I undergo this process, my guides will play the song, "I can see clearly now the rain is gone" to me in my head. When I hear that glorious tune, I know they are telling me, "ok Jules, we have enough info here, it's time for the shift." The shift meaning, intentionally shifting my focus, energy, and attention to the healing and away from the wound. I can't go back and change the past; neither can you. That is not where your point of power is. Lao Tzu says, "when you are depressed, you are living in the past, when you are anxious you are living in the future, when you are at peace, you are living in the present."

The present moment is the point of power. It is our point of power in transformation, in attraction, and then creation. When we change or transform, we vibrate at a different energy level, we change our point of attraction and what we create is new and different. Wasn't it Einstein who said the definition of insanity was doing the same things over again and expecting a different result? What we create will be consistent with the new way we feel within. So, we can't fool the universe or God by saying affirmations or prayers. God is responding to how you feel and who you are. This is why it's so important to allow ourselves to feel better. To seek out feeling better. Once we have gathered the information we need, we can begin to build anew. Healing doesn't come in simply going back and plucking the weeds. Healing comes as we build anew. When we shift our focus and attention toward our wellbeing. And when we get excited for all the new patterns of behavior, and when we commit to them, we will shift into the vibration of our own wellbeing.

How many times have you gone back and gone over a painful experience, only to come to the same conclusion? How many times have you said the words, I forgive, I let this go, only to relive it again and again? Because it is not in saying the words "I forgive" and "I let go" that any of that actually happens. It is in feeling the energy and vibration of forgiveness and feeling like it no longer holds you prisoner, that all becomes true. The problem with forgiveness, that keeps people stuck, is that they confuse it with access. Forgiveness is an energy, a state of being. Access means allowing what caused the injury access to you at the same level. If access prevents forgiveness, then this is a physical boundary problem, not an energy problem. Create the boundary and watch how the energy then has the space to transform! We have been conditioned to believe that space and distance are "wrong." If two people are having friction every time they are together and you create distance between them, the friction ends. With no further catalyst for the friction, the energy can change. Have you ever had a disagreement with someone only in a few days to feel completely fine and it no longer matters to you? That is because you created space and distance to get clarity and transform the energy. Once you transform your energy you get to decide what that "access" looks like for you in the future. The more you cultivate your energy and your state of being, it will become sacred. You will realize that not everyone can or will align with it in the ways they used to. That's ok. That does not need to steal anything away from love. Love defies space and distance. And sometimes it needs it to thrive! The more you begin to lean away from all those people and patterns that have kept you stuck in your unwellness, and lean toward the people and patterns that promote your wellness, the stronger and more healed you will feel.

Don't fool yourself into thinking that each time you revisit the past, you are just "venting" or getting it out a little more. That is your ego telling you that. Once you get the wisdom or the "nectar" from a situation, going back is just a reinvestment of your energy. It is recreating the wheel of the past. That is your ego's attempt to keep you stuck in that same old story where outcomes are predictable, and turmoil feels familiar and "safe." The truth is, the more energy you invest in it, instead of changing it, the more the past will stay on repeat. Your time, your energy, and your focus are your greatest currency. Use them to build your platform to healing. You may be saying, "Julie, that is not easy. If we don't talk about it, how do we get it out?" You can absolutely talk about it. When you do, create a new conversation around the wellbeing you've achieved from it. What epiphanies did you find about yourself? What truths were you able accept as a result? What are you now trying to do differently? What is helping you feel better now that you are going to do more of as a result? What places did this shed light on? What did it give to you, instead of what it took from you? What new goals and desires were born within you as a result?

This is how we flip the script and change the storyline in forward motion. When you find yourself triggered, hold space and time for those emotions to be felt and then allow them to move until there is relief. Sometimes I can do this in minutes. Then lean into one of the tools that you know makes you feel better. Not in an emotionally bypassing kind of way, like it never happened. In a way that acknowledges what you've been through and how you continue to soothe yourself when needed and keep moving forward. If you want to talk to someone about it, change the dialogue. "I was triggered today, I felt this emotion, but I went for a walk, and I meditated, and I started to feel better. You know, I am getting better and better at this every minute of every day. I recovered from my trigger even quicker this time around. I released the emotions that weren't serving me quicker than I ever had done before." See how this feels different? No longer blaming the people or conditions in our lives that we can't change, but taking responsibility and knowing we don't need to give our power away to those things.

The truth is, there are many people and conditions you will need to accept that you cannot change. Investing your energy there will only continue to disempower you. Once you start investing your energy in accepting that and changing your experience of those things, you will feel much more empowered because those things are not dictating your life experience anymore- you are! So, you see, it never really was a breakdown, it was a breakthrough!

JULIE CLAPP

REFLECTIONS & NOTES CHAPTER 7

Chapter 8

"If you want to awaken all of humanity, awaken all of yourself. If you want to eliminate suffering in the world, then eliminate all that is dark and negative in yourself. Truly the greatest gift you have to give is that of your own self transformation." ~Lao Tzu

One of the greatest parts of my healing journey was when I realized how much it tied into everything else in my life. I realized how it had held me back for so many years. It was when I really started to get into manifestation that I started to realize the parts of me that needed healing. Manifestation happens when your energy aligns with the energy of what you are desiring or sometimes even what you are not desiring. So, as I prayed for things to change, I was shown what I needed to change within to heal my vibration. I started to see my journey full circle as if I was not a willing participant, but a spectator watching a movie.

As I mentioned, I had a lot of anxiety in my younger years. I grew up as the youngest of nine siblings in an Irish

Catholic household. The end. Just kidding. Although due to our age gaps we didn't all live in the same home all at once; to call the energy "chaotic" at times was an understatement. We lived in a four-bedroom raised ranch with one bathroom. Ironically, I believe this is also what made us so close. My parents had their fair share of burdens, I very much looked at them like superheroes. While I won't share their entire stories because they are not my stories to tell, I will give a little background that shaped that view of my parents.

My mom grew up with very little money, went to parochial school and spent some of her childhood years in foster care. I never heard her say one bad thing about her parents. She always spoke of them highly and from a place of love and compassion. She taught me forgiveness like no other figure on this earth. My dad's father died in a tragic accident when he was just 13. He was the oldest boy of nine! He joined the navy and walked every one of his sisters down the aisle. No doubt practice for all the years he then walked each of his seven daughters down the aisle. My dad shared with me a story of when he went to fortune teller years ago. She told him he would be surrounded by a lot of women in his life, and to beware Friday the 13th. He had a boating accident years later on Friday the 13th that nearly killed him! And he was indeed surrounded by women in his life- six sisters and seven daughters. Early on my dad struggled with alcoholism, and I share that because if he were here today, he would proudly share that. See, my dad became known as "The Closer" at all of his AA meetings. He traveled speaking to youth groups and adolescents about the gifts of sobriety. He took many under his wing. He hosted an AA meeting at my house a week prior to his passing. He was dedicated to it. When I watched him speak, I witnessed God working through him and so did everyone in that room. On my darkest days I would think of the things my parents had overcome in their life, and not to gaslight my pain, but to know that somewhere inside me was the cloth of those same capes God had weaved with them. I just did not realize it until years later.

I had decided at an early age that I would not contribute to any chaos in my household, I would leave that to my older siblings. Now it is possible that this was a subconscious effort on my part to be seen as the "perfect child," but nonetheless I strived to attune to the needs of others early on. At a very young age I had learned to be hyper-attuned to the energy in my environment. I had no idea at the time what I was doing, but my ability to "read a room" proved to be very useful in making me feel safe, and as it turns out, helped me create a full-time career for myself years later. Empaths are sensitive to energy, so getting a read on energy early on, or being hypervigilant, made the environment more predictable in my mind, so it felt safer and like I had more control. I realize now that I had more anxiety in my nursing years because it was a very unpredictable environment. I became a complete control freak to feel safe. The constant stressful stimuli in that environment became increasingly more difficult for me to control the deeper I went into my mediumship. Essentially, I was sensitizing myself in order to read people on some days and then on other days putting on a suit of armor to shield my energy field.

That job taught me surrender on so many levels. It taught me to allow discomfort and uncomfortable emotions, but not until I left. While I was there, I very much tried to control those things. It wasn't until I started my career as a medium that I was able to see that more clearly. I liken it to a turtle shedding its shell. You feel a little soft, unprotected, and vulnerable. In order to be a medium, I had to allow myself to become sensitive to stimuli. The intuitive voice is called the still small voice for a reason. In order to turn up the volume, you have to become sensitive to sound, feeling, touch, taste, smell, vision. All of your senses heighten. So, the way you interact with the world changes too. Our senses in the physical world translate to the nonphysical. In essence, we use the same senses to communicate and connect with spirit as we do as a human being, just in a different way. This is what is called ascending from a third dimensional experience to a fifth dimensional experience. Kids we are upping our game to 5D.

You know how when you were a kid and would go to the movie theatre to see a 3D movie? You put those glasses on and voila, the screen starts to pop out to you in a whole new reality. That is the same thing that happens when you heighten your senses. Most people go through the world using their physical senses. Their sight is dependent on what they physically see in front of them, but that is not their only sense of vision. Clairvoyance is another way for us to clearly "see" from a 5th dimensional point of view. When you daydream, you are looking at images playing in your mind's eye. This is your clairvoyant space. My guess is if you started to pay attention to what it was you were daydreaming, you would realize that daydreams are not always as they appear. They are often not logical and seemingly out of the blue. When this happens it is because what you are seeing in your clairvoyant space is more than likely images that are not being generated from your logical mind. It is from a higher consciousness which could include your own intuitive voice, or higher self, or spirit. Spirit meaning, loved ones in heaven, your higher power, angels, and guides. Similarly, we have many other 5th dimensional senses as well.

Claircognizence is "clear knowing." Just as you can download a file from your computer, you can download full thought or story blocks of knowing through your claircognizence. Have you ever been having a conversation with someone, and you just know you are meant to share a certain story in your experience with them, but are not sure why? When you do the person says that they needed to hear that. You are both left dumbfounded as to why you felt guided to do that. That is your claircognizence. A parallel story or experience popped into your head out of the blue because on some level your higher-self picked up on the energy of the person and what was needed at that time. Clairaudience is another sense that develops with awakening the senses. It is clear hearing. That song that pops into your head without any logical reason, but yet with ironically relevant significance to life in that moment in time, yeah that is your clairaudience. Have you ever heard the thoughts in your head as your voice speaking to you without a logical reason of why they are popping in? That's your clairaudience too! These are all ways we can hear with our inner sense of hearing. Clairsentience is clear feeling. When I connect with spirit, I feel different. Sometimes I feel a different emotion or personality that does not correlate to my current emotional state or my own personality. I may feel irritable or sometimes even overly elated, or anxious. This is because another energy other than my own is impressing like a fingerprint on my energy field or aura. I call the aura the "buffer zone." It's the spongy matter between us that protects our energy field from the energy outside of us, but will inevitably absorb some of that worldly energy in the process. This causes us to feel that energy. Sometimes depending on the strength of the energy that is being impressed on me, it can make me physically feel things as well. If a spirit had lung issues, I may actually feel difficulty breathing or that I need to cough. This sensation typically does not last because it takes a tremendous amount of energy for spirit to communicate in this way. Once I acknowledge it, it usually starts to diminish and go away. It is just a means to get my attention and say what they want me to say. Other senses are also clear taste and clear smell. Using your sense of taste, or clairgustance, on a 5th dimensional level is when you taste something without actually having consumed it. Clairalience is clear smelling. Ever smelled the smell of cigarette smoke, coffee, or the perfume or cologne that reminds you of a particular loved one in spirit without anyone or anything actually being around to have caused the smell? This is your clairalience in full effect.

Most of us usually have one or two senses that we are dominant with. Similar to be left or right-handed. It is what comes natural to us. As a medium I have learned that no matter which of our 5D senses we are more dominant in, we can improve our reception and sensitivity of the others with exercises, time, and commitment. So how is this relevant to healing? Well, on my mediumship journey I realized there are so many people in the world that are also empaths. I have channeled so many spirits that had suffered depression and anxiety in this physical world and came through to say they too were empathic, an energy sponge. They had no awareness of it and no idea how to process all the stimuli, so unfortunately it became an edge of their sword that got the best of them in their life on this earth. When my journey of awakening started, I noticed that my senses were becoming a lot more heightened. The more aware I became of these changes, the stronger they became. When I would be in groups of people it became nearly impossible for me to not be barraged with a multitude of stimuli on all levels. Now I've learned how to harness this, but in the beginning I didn't. The more I started to commit to connecting to spirit on a more regular basis, these senses became a lot more heightened. I was sensitizing myself on all levels and I wasn't even realizing it; my nervous system responded accordingly. I became more sensitive to the physical world too, sounds, feelings, touch, etc. This was so important in my development as a medium because I needed to be able to recognize the difference in my own thoughts, feelings, and emotions, and that of others. As a sensitive I became a sponge that would pick up a lot on the energy around me; it's how I learned to read the room. This is why many people experience psychic phenomenon as a child. The process of hyper-attunement to energy starts there. Not only that, but children don't have veils yet. Veils are layers that separate what we learn from physical experience and the consciousness of our soul. This is why children experience spirit so clearly, until we add in fear and conditioning and tell them what is "not real." I learned very quickly the importance of protecting my energy, and becoming consciously aware of how I was affected by energy impressing on me, whether that be from human beings or spiritual beings. Both are equally powerful in effecting our energy.

Here's the most important golden nugget here: it is a lot easier to set boundaries with spiritual beings than human beings! Any nonphysical energy that makes me uncomfortable is so easily removed from my energetic field. I know and believe in my power to do that. Human energy is a lot more difficult to navigate. Have you ever said to someone, "I'm gonna have to ask you to leave because your energy makes me extremely uncomfortable?" #awkward. Here's the truth bomb though. Once you are aware that this is happening, which my guess is that it is, if you are reading this, you are responsible for your energy. It is no longer acceptable to play the blame game. It is your job to have an awareness of your energy as well as that of others. To use these senses to help you navigate energy more responsibly and wisely. Also, to realize that as energetic exchangers, it is necessary to constantly tend to and heal ourselves. We are always picking up energy from the physical world and from the spiritual world. The difference between an individual that experiences life on a 3D level versus a 5D level is merely our awareness of it. Most people are just walking around miserable, in bad moods, thinking they have that black cloud following them around, with no realization of their power to heal, release and renew themselves.

Here's another truth nugget you are now ready for: we are all empaths. People that call themselves that are just aware of the concept of energy and how they dance with it. They can on some level differentiate between their own energy and the energy of others. They know how to interpret energy using their 5D senses and they are learning to heal themselves and are inadvertently healing the world and others as a result. The rest of the world just has not yet discovered that they are an energetic sponge. They have not developed their 5D senses, which in some ways inhibits their ability to pick up on nonphysical stimuli, and in other ways makes them more vulnerable to energy because they have less awareness of it. No doubt if you are reading these words, you are an empath, and you know it. You are already using your 5D senses to some degree, you just might need a little help fine tuning them to your advantage. As an empath it is critical that you make a commitment to tending to your energy and to healing it on a consistent basis. A wounded empath is a disempowered angel. You came here because your spirit and your creator believed in your ability to learn to navigate these God-given gifts and abilities. You are a purposeful soul that is needed to heal and as a result you will inevitably inspire others to do the same. Only in states of healing can we influence the healing of others in a positive way instead of a negative way. Kahlil Gibran says, "your pain is the breaking of the shell that encloses your understanding." As an empath you may feel things to a greater degree, to a deeper depth, but remember, depth is proportionate to height. As you heal your wounds you unlock greater awareness, greater understanding, greater levels of sensitivity, greater grace, greater compassion, greater love, and greater purpose. This is what you came here for! You came here not with the promise of a pain free life. You came here knowing that your sweet little soul would feel on all levels and that you would take those feelings and learn how to use them to empower you, to teach you, to heal you and to bring that healing into the world at a time when it is so needed.

REFLECTIONS & NOTES CHAPTER 8

Chapter 9

"The Wounded Empath is a Brave Warrior in Disguise" ~ Me

In my darkest moments writing became an emotional form of release, healing, and self-expression. It was a way to feel seen and safe at the same time. In my last book "Waking Jules" I described the process of awakening to my mediumship abilities and the challenges that ensued as a result. Spirit divinely guided me when to start writing this book, ironically as I did, I went through another awakening in real time. And it was far more challenging than I ever anticipated. As I said before, it was when the pandemic started that my anxiety seemed to be triggered to a new level. Not only within me, but everywhere around me. As an empath I immediately wanted to retreat. Relationships felt harsh and I was not sure if it was due to my state of being, the state of others, the world or all of it. Nonetheless, it felt increasingly more overwhelming to try to cultivate feelings of safety and security within my physical body. My anxiety was at an all-time high and my nervous system felt weary. I think it's important to express that great things can be born out of some of our darkest moments. There is always a reciprocal expression of light and dark within us at each given moment. That is our duality, and I had already come to learn that I was only able to access those deeper truths in my darkness. So, into the darkness I went again.

From the start of the pandemic in spring 2020 through spring 2023 I experienced what you've probably heard many people in the spiritual community call "The Dark Night of the Soul." I had always viewed myself as a "love and light girl," but in the depth of my dark night, that became a concept I started to find so "new agey" for lack of a better label, and toxically positive. Before this time, it was unfathomable to me that there would be a day where this love and light girl could awake one day to feel empty, devoid of emotion, and completely apathetic toward life. I mean for years I had defined myself as the girl that woke up, sometimes anxious, but mostly looking forward to the mystery of the day and the blessing of my morning coffee. I was having a hard time bridging the gap to understand how that girl, who had already defined herself as "awakened" could feel that way.

Dark night of the soul was an understatement. The level of fear that I felt in response to this apathy was immeasurable and somewhat indescribable. The best way I can describe it is a feeling as though someone I deeply love and care about had died. Someone that I was deeply dependent on had dissolved from physical existence. I felt a deep sense of grief. The kind of grief that makes you apathetic to life's blessings and joy. The kind of grief that creates numbness and is completely anhedonic. The kind of grief that makes you nauseous and anxious when you first awaken because of the uncertainty of it. The only thing that I was certain of on that morning was that my mind, my body, and my spirit were telling "the healer" within me that she had more healing to do. Without fully understanding what I needed to heal from. There was no death. There was no big catastrophic event other than the pandemic that was a catalyst. In actuality, I came to realize that it had been a slow and steady process of degrading and dishonoring my needs that led me to that moment. I thought having realized I had been a people pleaser and done so much work, was the work. How could there be more? There was. So much more. What I know now is that there was actually a death that occurred that day. It was a great friend, and a protector. It was someone I relied on for many years. It was another layer to my veil, another part of my ego. Even as I wrote these words, I did so with no intent to fool you into thinking that my healing is done or that I have it all figured out. For now, I know that healing is not a destination to be achieved, and it can only truly be defined by how we feel in a moment. I have accepted healing as a constant in the evolution of my soul. It no longer needs to look like what we've been conditioned to believe. It doesn't have to be curled up in a ball, avoiding life, and sucking our thumb in bed, although I may have done that from time to time. Most people in my life never even knew that I went through this. I came to this realization that there was a fighter in me, but I had yet to get to know her well enough apparently. My hope is as I share my discovery of her, these words help you to reach for that fighter if you experience a dark night, too.

I remember crying in the depth of pain and trying to explain to my husband how I was feeling. I imagine the fear it instilled in him to see his stoic wife who liked to play the role of the "know it all" and always found the answers, had none and was in a complete state of fear. I could see his fear. I could also see the fear in my mother's eyes. To a mother witnessing a child in pain, what a mother hears is, "it's my fault," "I did something wrong," "I didn't protect you," and "how can I fix this?". In these moments I prayed for help in trying to express myself to the people I love with grace in a time I felt devoid of it. But I wasn't devoid of it. I said to my mom,

"Remember when you took care of dad when he was ill?"

She said, "yes."

I asked her, "was that hard and emotionally taxing to you?"

"Yes," she replied again.

"Did you feel as though you had to heal from that?"

"Yes," she said solemnly.

My final question, "Did you blame dad?"

"No," she said in an "of course not" tone.

I said, "then why must you believe I blame you for my pain or hold you responsible for my healing?" I think in that moment she realized this was a journey she had no control over as a mother. My expression of pain was so different this time, than it was when my dad died. I honored that my emotional state was revealing to me a deep need to heal not from one particular event like a death of someone I love, but from all the parts of me that I was ready to let go of and lovingly grieve. It was a deep need to heal from years of allowing my ego to distance me from myself through all of life's events. The more we undergo the process of healing, especially in an awakened state, the quicker we seek truth, instead of relying on our ego to protect us. Essentially, each time, we are becoming aware of another layer of our ego self to reveal more of our conscious self. So, while there may have been people in my life that triggered me, they shone a spotlight on my pain. At this level of awareness, I felt no need or urge to blame them, but I did distance myself from them. I felt as though they were just the catalysts and willing participants to show me the deepest and darkest corners of myself that needed my attention. The largest misdirection of energy in the healing process is when we then take our focus and direct it back on the people and the experiences that shone that spotlight, instead of directing on what the spotlight revealed to us. The apathy that was revealed to me in this depth, was one I had never felt before, ever. But because I had been through an awakening before, I knew I could do it. Even with this new depth, I knew there was a new height available to me if I was willing to fight for it. And I did. I got to work. I knew I could heal this. And if you are uncertain of your ability to heal, this is why I'm writing this for you. I know you can heal, and I know God put me on this earth to say those words to you.

The next component was being willing to peel back the layers. Yes again, that is what healing is, peeling back the layers to what is at the core, over and over again. What I realized as "miss positivity" is that I allowed myself to spiritually bypass myself and tried to constantly sustain the higher vibrations I knew how to access and were always available to me. I conditioned myself to think, "why allow low vibrations if we don't have to?". This is what spirit revealed to me this time around. In my pain, I had some of the most beautiful readings. At the end, many of my clients were often crying and in a state of complete vulnerability. People telling me they were so grateful that we crossed paths and how I have helped them in their life. I thought wow, I needed to hear that, but I really didn't. I shed the part of my ego long ago that relied on the words of others to lift me up. When you allow others to build you up, you will also allow them to tear you down. When you know who you are, you don't allow either. What I did get out of it this time, what I needed to learn this time, is that alignment is not about feeling good or "high vibes" all the time! Yes, it's good to feel good, but in allowing ourselves to feel the depth of emotion, we also have so much power and alignment of our soul available to us if we try. Carl Jung says, "One does not become enlightened by imagining figures of light, but by making the darkness conscious."

I received the answer to one of the greatest mysteries of time. The question people ask me in all of my healing workshops and teachings regarding healing, spirit, and manifestation is: How do we maintain our vibration? Alignment isn't just about maintaining the high vibes, it's about keeping your heart open and connecting to God even when your emotional launching pad feels low! Even when you are feeling the lowest emotions on the vibrational scale, being in a state of allowance. When I started to peel back the layers of this apathy, underneath were the emotions that terrified me to feel. They were the lowest emotions on the vibrational scale. I realized spirit was cleansing me as I was able to fight to honor this lower layer of my ego. The message wasn't about "do your best to sustain." It was, "Julie, if you can allow yourself to feel the emotions you fear the most, then my dear, what is left to fear?". And so my journey to feeling began.

JULIE CLAPP

REFLECTIONS & NOTES CHAPTER 9

Chapter 10

"Jesus calling"

As I said before, writing has always been a way for me to soothe myself. One day after I meditated and prayed to Jesus, I channeled this automatic writing. I share this with you not in accordance with the religious dogma with which I was conditioned, but to share one of the greatest healers I connect with in spirit, every day: Jesus. And to let you know Jesus is there for us all, no matter what religion, race or creed. I hope it serves you.

"In conquering fear, thy will is done through me. For to be a healer one must only believe, and it shall be. With this comes great responsibility. To speak the word with gentleness and grace, for all who seek it feel broken. To know broken and to have healed broken is to have the ability to heal. Many will come. Discern where thy energy is best served. Some will want it, but do not need it. For all shall be led to the healer within. Take great self-care. Preserve thy self in wellness and it is wellness that shall be. Pay no mind to the seemingly "faithless," for all shall come to know faith through me. Hold my hand always each day and you shall never be led astray. Fear not what is to come, for miracles abound the earth when love dispels fear. Let

Love lead. When you fear the serpents, the serpents shall come. When you see not the serpents, the serpents cannot exist. Something without existence can have no power over you. Select what you breathe life into and give power to. In stillness and silence lies your strength and your holiness. Master your "Wholeness." And you shall master all else."

There have been people on my journey that I wrote about in my last book that have remained integral parts to my journey. Maureen Hancock, "The Medium Next Door" has trademarked as part of her work, "YOU NEED TO FEEL IT TO HEAL IT." She also told me that I was never really meant to be a nurse. She told me that on some level my soul knew I was meant to help people and nursing was an obvious choice, but I was really going to help people through mediumship. Even the psychic in me never could have predicted that this is where I would be led all these years later. Maureen's words of "feeling to healing" were never more relevant to me at this time of my dark night. Instead of me recycling off these words to all my clients, I was soaking them in myself. As I peeled back the layers, I realized that my soul had in some way incarnated into this world to heal ancestral wounds. I knew because I had been visited by some of my ancestors on the other side that told me this. And my response, was "why the fuck did I do that?!" LOL. No joke. So, I looked at the people closest to me whom I had witnessed healing or lack thereof for guidance. I took from that the qualities that inspired me the most and the qualities that pained me the most. I realized I had developed a belief system through my ancestral lineage that "hurt people, hurt people." I've even spouted that off in many of my healing workshops because in the moments I believed that, it was my path of least resistance. It was my ego fast tracking me to the quick fix. Instead of feeling the discomfort of emotions from watching those we love in pain, and the behaviors that go along with it, we can just make that quick peace and move on. We can avoid grieving the illusion of what we want to be and accepting what is. Alleviating ourselves of any work or discomfort in the process. But the cycles will always repeat. So that was a truth for me at that leg of my journey, but it is no longer. Now spirit said I have a new truth available to me, because I'm willing to go to that new layer and depth of emotional awareness and consciousness.

The truth is, that is bullshit. Hurt people don't hurt people. Hurt people who buy into the separateness of pain, instead of the grace of God within them, displace and project their pain on the people they love, on the vulnerable who they think will allow it to alleviate their discomfort. As a result, they perpetuate the cycle of pain. Essentially disconnecting themselves from their higher self, source, and God within them. Hurt people that hurt people, take the spotlight that has been shone on their pain and redirect it to all the people in their life instead of looking within. Hurt people that take that spotlight and lean into the grace of God within them for healing do great things. Only from a position and vibrational standpoint of "healing" can we be "healers," or be able to have any power to lead others to their healing. So, every single person that is in pain has a choice. Finger point, blame and project, in order to release the pain, or feel the discomfort, remove the fear of it, and start to notice what your pain is teaching you about yourself. Love your darkness into the light or create more darkness. This is shadow work.

As the grace of God that you call upon within you to rise up begins to flow, you start to receive amazing downloads of understanding and consciousness that help you too to rise! There is no time for misguided and misdirected focus toward another. There is only time to heal. Hurt people who are brave enough to keep their heart open, are actually in a very powerful position to bring healing to the world through their journey of healing. We do this not by making excuses for our behavior and allowing our ego to justify it in order to protect ourselves from the discomfort. We show up. We feel the depth of uncomfortable emotion and we take responsibility for why they may be showing up for us. This is to heal gracefully. We don't in turn release our pain by trying to make the people in our lives feel the same pain. That is the stuff that creates ancestral pain cycles that exist in family lines for years and generations to come. We each get to decide if that buck stops with us. Instead, let's choose to be brave and feel the pain and allow whatever we need to feel. I feel no need for blame or to hurt another in my process of healing. God has already shown me, it's not about others, they are just the mirror to lead me to more of me. Ironically, at this very same time my 16-year-old son said to me as I was telling him he shouldn't probably wear his faded and worn-out gym shorts that look like pajamas to school, "mom, it's not about other people." It's always us against ourselves! Isn't it though?

In the journey of us against ourselves and the grief of letting go of the layers of our ego and false sense of self and protection, there is a graceful healer in each of us yearning to blossom. Longing to be discovered, unleashed, and celebrated in all its glory! God planted that seed within us at the time of birth and lined up all the people along the way that were meant to shine the spotlight on those dark corners of your pain. We unfortunately don't get to decide the circumstances under which they will do that. All so that we can see it and give attention to it, not so that we could beat up those that shone it to us. Your attention and focus lie on watering those seeds. As you do the graceful healer blooms. The fear of discomfort dispels and dismantles in the darkness and the spotlight only makes the light of your heart shine brighter. This is the truth of who you are and who I am. This is our oneness. No need to let one another off the hook or keep one another on the hook. Neither have any impact. The only point of impact is either through perpetuating the pain or perpetuating the healing. This is the choice between perpetuating the fear or perpetuating the power of God within us. Perpetuating the light or perpetuating the darkness. An external war is really just an internal battle in disguise.

In choosing to let the wounded empath in me heal, I had to first recognize that what I was doing to sustain myself was not enough. First, I reminded myself of how I was speaking to myself. Remember when I was saying to the people in my life, "I'm broken" after my dad died? This time I chose differently. I chose to say I'm in need of healing, and I'm doing it. I knew my power to heal, and I chose to believe in it more than I bought into the illusion of the depth of pain within me. So first I came clean with the people in my life. I told them I needed space and time to heal and to not take it personally. I had been feeling like a fishing bobber that was mostly above water but easily pulled below the surface of wellbeing. It was so difficult for the sleeping people pleaser and perfectionist in me to say, "I'm depressed." I wanted to be the conditioned version of the perfect woman that had been created in the minds of many by the patriarchy lifetimes ago. The woman who could do it all and be stoic and not crack under pressure, and emotion, with no need to ever show it! The magnificent martyr and rescuer. What if that is what I needed to heal? Letting go of this ideologic definition of the woman I kept trying to be instead of just allowing myself to be who I was. What if I just needed to allow those beliefs to be dismantled so that the true me could emerge? I think it was hard for me to say I was anxious and depressed also because anyone who viewed my life from the outside would probably say, "she seems to have it all, how is she depressed?". I get this too! There is a fine line of victimhood and being blinded to the blessings in our lives when there are so many that are less fortunate. But I intuitively knew that if I told myself that at that moment, I would have been spiritually bypassing myself. That is when you tell yourself or someone else that it is wrong to feel any emotion without proper justification, according to either your or societal standards. That is the biggest load of crap! Perspective is a gift and many incarnated as suffering souls give it to us at times, but when we constantly deny ourselves the ability to feel uncomfortable emotions, we eventually become emotionally detached. We become apathetic.

Apathy results from depriving ourselves of our full range of emotion. So, as we deprive ourselves of feeling the lows, we rob ourselves of the highs!! That was why I was feeling apathetic. I told myself based on years of conditioning, that it was wrong to feel certain emotions, that they were not justified. It is right and just to feel any emotion that you feel. No need to get caught up in seeking external validation and understanding of them either. That will then become another layer to heal. To put it simply, expecting understanding from others to any vibrational state we are in, is an unattainable and unsustainable expectation because we are all constantly evolving and changing. It will eventually be revealed as disappointment in relationships. There will be times when people will vibrationally line up with your emotions and experiences and will therefore validate them for you, but this is not the healing work, even though it makes us feel better. This only temporarily satisfies the ego and over time if we become dependent on external validation to feel better, it will breed codependency. The truth is we don't need understanding or acceptance, we want it. What we need is love. And love can exist amidst misunderstanding. I found that for me it was not a basic need, it was a basic block to my own self-love. My guess is you've felt a lack of acceptance from someone in your life at some point? My other guess is you were able to leave that person behind and did not allow that person to shape the definition of who you were. If anything, that experience probably made you believe in yourself even more. The more we come into loving and accepting ourselves, the less we seek that on the outside from the people in our lives.

The truth is, only two people who are in exact vibrational alignment with their higher-self can authentically and truthfully express understanding. How often do you think that actually happens because people have the emotional maturity and capacity, versus how often people are just trying to make you feel "seen, and heard, and validated" as the current culture is calling for? What we are actually calling for is more compassion please, more grace please, more light please in a world that screams otherwise. The truth is, that all must start within first, then it shall transpire without. Most of external validation stems from places of obligation, expectation, and political correctness, not from true authentic alignment and understanding. And as energetic beings, we feel when it's authentic and when it's not. When we sacrifice our authenticity to satisfy an expectation, we detach from our higher selves and truth to meet another where they are. In times of heated emotions and triggers, we are often in our ego and that is when we tend to seek validation, so is validating someone in their ego actually compassionate or is it keeping them stuck in their ego? You can honor another's feelings without compromising truth. Much of my healing came from the people in my life, not meeting me in my ego and validating me. In fact, much came from them challenging my perspective in heated emotional moments. Helping me to learn the art of self-soothing, self-validation, self-acceptance, and self-reliance, shifting away from seeking acceptance, approval, blaming, and giving away all of my power to those outside of me.

When you learn to validate the self, you will be in a light that can help others learn to validate themselves instead of seeking it. It always lies within. Seeking it means asking others to temporarily separate from their higher selves to meet you where you are. It is the inner child begging for approval to feel what it feels. Learning to hold your inner child fosters a confidence in self within, thereby radiating self-confidence to others. These are the building blocks of healed and authentic relationships. Not those built on the shaky foundations and the shallow bonds of inauthentic validity. Standing in your light becomes challenging when you are faced with the choice of making another "feel better" instantly or challenging them to truly "feel better" by going within. People may initially view this as a lack of empathy or support, even self-centered. The truth is it is being centered in self. When you are centered in self you know that your alignment is your greatest point of power and so you need not sink into the ego to meet another in theirs. When you do, you only fuel the illusions of their ego and their separateness within themselves. True empathy can only exist from the higher self. When it stems from the ego it is a manipulative attempt at bonding at the level of ego. This is emotional bonding, or codependency, and it is a surface bond that will not withstand the tests of time and evolution, because eventually one party will heal, will connect with their higher self, and will receive the clarity of the soul, and so the process of dismantling the illusionary bond will begin. This is hallmark of why unhealthy relationships don't last. True bonds are formed when two parties are actually centered in self enough to hold their light and hold space for others to join them there, essentially, "we no longer meet down there, we meet up here."

REFLECTIONS & NOTES CHAPTER 10

Chapter 11

"The Last Shaman"

After "coming out" with my depressed emotions, my next step was to make my needs known. As an empath and a people pleaser it was always hard for me to make my feelings known without feeling guilty for doing so. In taking the brave step to let the people I love know what I needed, I set myself up to not feel resentment. Making your needs known without expectation creates the safest environment for healing. You are voicing your needs without an expectation that anyone who is not available or in the energetic space to do so will not. Meaning I knew that in order for me to heal, I could not expect others to self-abandon themselves for me to do so. I had already learned that! My needs of others were actually a lot simpler. They were- give me time, give me privacy to feel and to not feel like I have to put on a good face, because I will. Don't take my healing personal, it doesn't have anything to do with you, and try not to ask me to explain it, because healing takes a lot of energy. I shared when I had the energy to give to sharing and without putting pressure on myself to explain. Safety is critical in healing. So making your needs known is critical in healing because you are setting your stage and environment. In addition, anyone who is not able to honor those needs, you may need to set boundaries with them. People with unhealthy attachment styles in relationships will try to make your healing about them; make it clear, it is all about you versus you! After doing this I said to my husband, "I know my self-care game is strong, I have had a routine that has kept me well for years, it no longer cuts it. I need more."

About nine months prior I had come across a documentary on Netflix called, "The Last Shaman." It was the story of a college boy named James who seemingly "had it all" according to societal standards. Both of his parents were reputable physicians at Mass General Hospital. He was clinically depressed and suicidal most days. His parents with all of their knowledge, wisdom and traditional western medicinal intervention could do nothing to help him. They felt powerless, as did he. As a last stitch effort, the boy decided to seek out a shaman in the jungles of Peru and stated to his family if it didn't work, he was giving himself a license to end his life and his suffering. He went to many different shamans and even tried Ayahuasca which is a hallucinogenic to release repressed emotions, to no avail. Finally, he traveled to a remote village. In this village he developed a close bond with the village shaman. The shaman used plants and the soil from the earth and music as his healing remedies. It took a year. In that year a light was reignited in James. He had no contact with his family at that time. They had no way of knowing if he was even alive. After the year he returned home. He reconnected with his parents in a way that he hadn't before because he had reconnected with himself. From a place of healing instead of from a place of pain. While he still battles emotions as we all do while in this body, he is not suicidal. He has an appreciation for life that he had lost somewhere along the way. He found his peace within him. It was shown to him through the grace of nature.

About six months after watching this documentary I came across a webinar that kept popping up on my Instagram feed as a sponsored ad. It was a webinar about shamanic plant medicine and healing. I was so intrigued I took the webinar, and it lit something up inside me. I've always planted a garden at my home and found it so therapeutic, but I couldn't help but think spirit was guiding me to more with this. Last year I planted sage and lavender, and I used them in creating healing candles with different intentions. I felt even more strongly to lean more in the directions of growing my own plants. I learned so much from this webinar that I was able to incorporate into my everyday spiritual practices with greater respect and understanding. I had always used white sage, an abalone shell and a large feather to cleanse my aura and my space. To be honest I learned it years ago from watching the Long Island Medium. I started because I thought, "oh this is what mediums do." Then I researched the meaning behind it. It was a native American ritual that involved calling in the great spirit through the four directions. I would call in the element of earth with the sage. I would call in the element of water with the shell. I would call in the element of air by fanning the smoke with an eagle feather and I would call in the element of fire by lighting the sage. This ritual creates the fifth element of life. I thought the story was so meaningful. When I took the webinar, I learned that it is actually much more respectful to the Great Spirit and the native American tradition to not be so commercialized with it. To use the plants from one's own environment. To use a feather that crosses your path. That is a gift from the great spirit that is to be honored.

My husband and I go for walks in nature at least three times a week. On our walks we started to come across an abundance of hawk and turkey feathers. Large hawk feathers started to pop up out of nowhere on the street! I saved them for my cleansing rituals and thanked the Great spirit. I have also started to grow more of my own plants for cleansing, as many more than just sage have cleansing properties. In turn I have discovered on a new level how we can discover our healing in the simplest everyday components of the environment around us! So, when I started to feel depressed, I immediately felt guided to lean into my new shamanic healing rituals where spirit had recently guided me.

I scoured the internet and called my health insurance company to seek out therapists. None of them resonated with me. Most of the accessible conventional therapists that were available had zero background in the realm of human consciousness and the evolution of the soul. Because so many are awakening to the soul's journey, this is something that the mental health community seemed to be lacking support in. I would love to see more of it incorporated into therapeutic treatment modalities of healing trauma. I started to feel deeply alone on this journey. I went on Instagram and I looked up the hashtag #Shaman. Listen, desperate times call for desperate measures. So, I looked through a few profiles and none of them resonated, but then one woman popped up. Antonia.

I clicked on her profile and immediately her words resonated with me. Her creed spoke to my soul. I saw that we had a mutual connection on Instagram. It was the woman who taught the plant medicine webinar I took months prior! Everything inside me said, "reach out to her." I went on her website, and she had an opening that week. I was open! I said, "I'm going for it."

I was nervous and excited. This is something I'd never done before. I didn't know what to expect. I'm a little Irish Catholic girl who talks to Jesus, how would this fair? I do the session and Antonia moves me to tears. She tells me that many lightworkers amidst the pandemic have found that their traditional self-care practices were just not enough. Many were feeling overwhelmed and depleted. We are expanders. As we expand, we need more to support ourselves. She said she has even reached out to her ancestors and mentors to guide and support her. Ok great, so I'm not as alone as I thought! In that moment, Antonia calls in The Great Spirit and I have the most amazing experience. It reignited my spark. She does her healing work and then tells me what she gets from my energy. She sees how I've felt disconnected from my higher self. She says, "you have strong intuition, and you use it so wisely for others, but you have been silencing it for yourself." She sees to my soul that my tendencies to put others before myself, to give more than I feel like I have to give, has led me to depletion and to abandon the guidance of my inner voice. She said, "you silence your intuition for those you love. You will ignore harmful behaviors and hold on to the potential you see in others instead of what they are showing you. I see that your solar plexus chakra or energy center is weakened because of this pattern, and it is weakening your third eye." She had no idea that I had been working on my people pleasing. I was astounded. She guides me to call back my power. I tell her what I saw as she did the healing.

I was by a campfire. With me was an older Native American gentleman with a headdress and a short native American woman. I felt like I knew them all of my life. They made me feel safe and secure and held, much like my guides do. We spoke no words, but I knew what they were saying. We were sitting by a fire. I was sweating. Profusely sweating, like a cleansing of sorts. The woman put her hand on my shoulder and guided me to see beyond the fire. In an instant it was like I was in the womb again. I was questioning if I was ready to incarnate into this life. The funny thing is my mom always called me her "jewel." She said I was the miracle baby. She was told after having an ectopic pregnancy that she wouldn't be able to have children. But here I am. I laughed at the thought that my little soul contemplated the challenge of this journey before I was born! Next, I witnessed myself at all different ages. At each age I showed up, the Native American woman had the now 44-year-old Julie, hug all of the other "Julie's." Each one I showed love to like a mother shows her child. In that moment I felt a self-love and acceptance rise within me like I had never known before. In that moment, nothing else mattered. It was a feeling of complete surrender and acceptance of myself, all of the versions of myself. I see a vision of a wolf and of a toucan. Antonia and I discuss their meanings. One is to rediscover the empowerment of my voice. Like a baby bird learning to sing; I was learning to fine tune the instrument that God gave me to play my greatest music in this world. The other, the wolf. Well, it was a symbol of fierce protection and bravery. Ironically, I had been noticing even the simplest acts of bravery in others around me and letting them know when I witnessed it. More than likely this was my inner voice trying to guide me to my own bravery, in following my instincts and not the "pack" or the crowd. A message that self-reliance and trusting the power of your own intuition, was the new brave!

The hardest part about being a psychic medium is not only being able to feel the pains of others, but to see so clearly the wounds beneath their aching hearts. The best part about being a psychic medium is being able to witness the journey of the rising, of the resiliency and of the healing. I might see your inner wounds, but I also see your inner warrior, I couldn't help but think, maybe it was time for me to meet mine. Antonia was the one to show her to me. The wounds beneath the surface of us all and our ability to be our own healers, is our oneness, not our separateness. My new native guide had just shown me that self-love and self-acceptance are the best medicine for our souls, for in heaven it's really all we know. So, when we feel lost, that is what makes us feel at home again while in these dense bodies. I've seen my warrior, and I see yours. This life is tough, and no one is escaping unscathed or unwounded. But we have the ability to heal. So, we can do this messy, or we can do this magically, beautifully and awe-inspiringly. If you're here my guess is you heard the call from God when he whispered to you, "show me your warrior."

In the next few weeks, I upped my self-care game significantly. I spent a lot of time in nature and calling on the Great Spirit to help me. I was guided each day to cleanse with the power of the elements and what nature was giving me. The vibration of nature is consistent with the vibration of our souls. Each day spirit would guide me to cleanse with earth, air, fire, and water. So, I would use sage, my hawk feathers, burn incense and take cleansing baths in my saltwater pool. I followed their guidance. Then one morning I went to do my message of the day on social media and my spirit guides told me to wait. So, my husband and I went walking as we usually do on the weekends, and I remember seeing my new Native American guide in front of me. I had been feeling anxious that morning for no particular reason, and movement of my body often releases those dense emotions from me. As I could feel my energetic shield dissolving, I heard my guide say, "It's ok, let it down, you are divinely protected." We learn through the ebbs and flow of pain and healing to develop these energetic shields to protect us at times. In that moment I was reminded we don't need them. They are just an illusion. We can't really protect ourselves from the pains of life. But what we can do is fully and wholeheartedly feel them and believe in our ability to rise and heal over and over again. Those shields block us and hold us back. It is with our hearts wide open that we discover the truth and authenticity of our soul and what it's capable of in this life.

I looked up as I got this message and there was a peep hole of sunlight shining through the clouds. I took a picture and posted it on my social media with the message. It looked like the shape of an angel with wings and arms spread wide open and a beam of light radiating from it all the way down to the ground. I knew why my guides told me to wait that morning to do my message of the day. They wanted me to share that message. The message that we are all divinely protected. There is someone in heaven always one step ahead gently guiding us through each bump in the road, hurdle, or mountain. That it was time not just for me, but for us all, as a collective to embrace our wounds, to empower our empathic angel within, to call on our inner warrior, to show ourselves so much love and acceptance that we lower our shield, shed the fears, raise our arms up high, open up our hearts and start shouting from the rooftops, "more love please!" For it's the only way to heal.

REFLECTIONS & NOTES CHAPTER 11

Chapter 12

"Little Jewels"

In the next weeks I continued to channel with The Great Spirit and with Jesus. More wounds were revealed to me, more layers of my ego were shedding, and I was coming into more and more of my authentic self. In one of my meditations, I recalled being with my two Native American Spirit Guides. We were standing facing a waterfall. It was beautiful and I had never seen it before. They motioned for me to look in the water. There was me, little Jules splashing and playing in the waterfall. They reminded me as a child I had a terrible fear of the water. I would love to be by it and in it but would cling to the edge of any pool and not let anyone come near me, even my dad who would try to teach me to swim. He was an amazing swimmer; I used to love to just watch him. Somehow my love for the water won the battle over that fear and I learned to swim. These guides said to me, all the while you were clinging to your safety, that is what your higher self, your inner child was doing. You were playing and splashing and dancing in the water. She was calling you toward love and away from fear. So, this is the truth in all of our situations. As we cling to control thinking we can protect ourselves from the worst, our inner child is dancing and splashing and playing. It is reminding us that control is an illusion, and so is fear. In acceptance of what is and our belief in our power to overcome anything that we deem "the worst," we surrender. We become joyful and playful and abundant. We learn to fall in love with whatever is right now.

My encounters with my Native American guides continued over the course of months following my shamanic healing session. They made me see more clearly how I could actually empower myself. In my moments of fear, anxiety and apathy, I was simply feeling disconnected from my higher self. It was calling me to feel all things. I realized that the only way was in the feelings, even the uncomfortable ones. My husband had been going to acupuncture for years. Though I had never been, I was fully in awe of the results my husband had. He had herniated discs in his neck with nerve root impingement. This means the protruding discs were pressing on nerves that extend out of his spinal cord. This caused pain, numbness, and loss of range of motion that impacted his work and his everyday quality of life. As we sought out traditional medical guidance, we were told that surgery was the only way. Now I'm a nurse. I had worked in a hospital for over 17 years. I had seen the results of such surgery and everything in my gut said this was not our course. My husband heard of this acupuncturist from a friend, and I encouraged him to try it. He stuck with it. There was no quick fix. Results were not instantaneous, but they came slowly. While we never repeated his MRI to see what had changed, all had changed. My husband no longer had pain. His full range of motion and sensation in his arms returned to full capacity. So, as I was learning to navigate my "dark night of the soul" I felt compelled to try acupuncture myself. My husband made an appointment for me, and I went.

On my first visit, I was greeted by Elizabeth and her sweet rescue pup B. Immediately I feel held and welcome. The energy was inviting and safe. I went into the treatment room and what I see on the wall is the exact sign I needed to let me know this is where I belong. On the wall are four pictures of the four elements of nature. Earth, Air, Fire and Water. "Thank you Great Spirit!" I utter to myself. I lay on the table for the first time and Liz proceeds to take my pulse in a Chinese Medicine way, not in a traditional western medicine way. She tells me that because I'm sensitive she is going to go slow with treatment. What she sees is that my energy is not grounded. My immediate reaction for someone who teaches grounding practices to others and prides themselves on their self-care routine, was how did I let this happen? She said, "you spend a lot of time connecting on an energy level. We need to define your edges. You need clear boundaries of where your energy ends and others' begin." This was one of the most profound epiphanies for me and something I totally needed to hear at the time. I am aware of boundaries, but this brought the realization that mine were clearly not strong enough. Ya see, I have a tendency to become easily enmeshed in others' energies. I'm a fixer, a control freak, a perfectionist, and a people pleaser. But now I know I'm actually none of those things. I'm none of those labels. Those were simply the names I gave all my protector parts. What I started to discover as I healed those wounds, was who Julie really was. My journey began to define my edges and to let others see clearly the boundaries of where I ended, hoping this will help them to define their edges too!

JULIE CLAPP

REFLECTIONS & NOTES CHAPTER 12

Chapter 13

"Why fit in when you were born to Stand out!"

~Dr. Seuss

I remember seeking out all the pages on Instagram that screamed "I can help with mid-life crisis stuff" on a soul level. Many of the pages resonated with my truths of the consciousness of our souls and many would post things that would trigger me from time to time. One particular thing that I noticed from traditional therapists that triggered me over and over again were reminding others how important it was to feel seen, heard, and validated in order to feel accepted and whole. I already knew innately this was about soothing the ego. So of course, it rubbed me the wrong way. In order to understand this more deeply, I had to realize why. I had to peel back the layers of this trigger. In all honesty, I validated people's feelings every day. I helped them to feel seen, to feel understood, every day in my work, but I did so from alignment and from the vibrational standpoint of my higher self, or spirit. It wasn't just about validating their experience, it was about getting them to align with the perspective of their higher self and at the level of their vibrational alignment.

Let me share with you my experience of how I came to this realization with spirit. As I stated before I'm the youngest of nine children. My mom who to this day will tell you she's 39 years old, tells me we were all immaculate conceptions. Ok Roni! She also thought for many years LOL meant lots of love! Imagine the havoc she wreaked on social media with that one. As the youngest child I learned very quickly how important it was to fly under the radar. To be seen and heard didn't seem so fun. So, I learned shy and introverted was the way to go. Sometimes, however, that became an obstacle. Sometimes, I wanted to be seen and heard. Sometimes, I wanted to be included in all the stuff my "cooler" older siblings were doing. So, I learned to maneuver this internal duality with clever manipulation. As a child around eight-years-old, my neighbors were the ages of my older siblings, teenagers, so they had a neighborhood gang that would all hang out from time to time. One of my neighbors had a pool and my older siblings would go over and swim, but because I wasn't able to swim yet, I was not able to without my parents. I would hide in the bushes surrounding the pool and peek at all the kids having fun, plotting and planning on how I would be seen and included. I've got it! I would run home and tell my mom, but that didn't work. She knew that she couldn't deprive her other children of experiences they were ready for simply because I wasn't. Darn, she was not manipulatable. Ok I'd have to work the other end then! I'd go back to my post in the bushes and yell to my brother and sisters, "You guys have to come home right away, mom wants you." Out of the pool they would scramble and rush home. By this time, I've found a secure place to hide. My plan worked, surely if I wasn't going to be included in the fun, they could not be allowed to have fun! Once they realized that I had made that story up, they were less than pleased with me. I learned very early, that manipulation, although it felt good to my ego to temporarily disturb their fun, did not work either. Still, I continued from time to time to play the game my ego had taught me. They would be invited into the neighbors' houses, and I would swiftly create the story line to either get myself invited or disrupt their fun! Sometimes, if I played the "I'm telling mom" game, I'd get invited in, other times I got the door slammed shut on me, which only made me more creative. I will say this, it never made me feel ill toward them, in fact it made me look up to them even more. Somehow, they knew how to feel "included." A quality I clearly emulated in them. It wasn't until recent years that I Iearned why.

Once I had the adult awareness that I was a people pleaser, I realized that too was a means to manipulate others to make me feel loved and accepted. Changing that meant learning how to please myself. Like the airline stewardess says, you must first put the oxygen mask on before you can save anyone else. Complete depletion and disconnection from myself brought me to the realization that I needed my oxygen mask. In doing what is best for yourself, you will inevitably disappoint people in your life. Especially those that have held on to that persona that you created for them. They will find it difficult to understand and may see you following your inner guidance as abandonment and even selfishness sometimes. You need to do it anyway. As I set these new boundaries of allowing myself to disappoint others in order to not disappoint myself, dishonor myself, or abandon myself, new depths and layers of wounding were revealed to me.

REFLECTIONS & NOTES CHAPTER 13

Chapter 14

"Settle down, it will all be clear." ~Phillip Phillips

When I came out of the medium closet, I felt extremely rejected by my religious community and even by some within my family. The community I had built my foundation upon. The community that I considered my safety net, my protection and had built my wellbeing upon. My Catholic Faith. I felt ousted by my people at the time I needed them the most. I was confused. My fragile ego needed them to validate me at that time. They didn't. In them not validating me, I realized that I too had created a perception of my community, my people. I cast their roles in their story to not be themselves, but to please and validate me when I needed it. It made me go within, directly to my source. To my God. Not the God that existed in that church. The God that existed in my church within. God reminded me of when I was a little girl seeking to be seen and validated by my siblings. They were reflecting a wound that I carried into this world to heal on a grander scale. So was my community now. Same wound, showing up in different people. I had an inclusivity wound.

A deep and profound inclusivity wound. Maybe I was a witch burned at the stake in a previous life, who knows. Maybe this life for me is about asking why society keeps focusing on the witches and not those who were burning them?

The truth is years ago my siblings were teaching me to go within to discover my validation, my safety, my security, and my acceptance. Ya see, when we learn to accept the darkest corners of ourselves that we have some way hidden from the world or rejected, we no longer seek acceptance from others. We feel accepted wherever we go. We don't need acceptance and we know it cannot be found in another. Understanding and acceptance as we said before are two separate things. Understanding is something our ego craves. That makes us feel included and accepted. Understanding is a vibrational variable. It can only be achieved when two beings are in complete vibrational alignment with one another. We don't have the same experiences and we don't have the same conditioning, so therefore no two people will experience things exactly the same way. When we expect understanding in order to feel accepted, we are setting ourselves up for isolation and disappointment. It is our inclusivity wounds that reveal to us, we do not fully accept ourselves. In my dark night of the soul, I realized that shame was an emotion that I avoided feeling my whole life. I needed to allow myself to feel it. It was not mine to carry. It was my emotional response to not feeling accepted as I did not accept myself. There were many people in my life, on social media, and in the Catholic community whose words and behavior made me feel shameful for expressing the truth of my consciousness, my soul, and my mediumship and it was time for me to do something about that.

Now I could simply blame everyone if I wanted to satisfy my ego, but I knew better. So, I meditated on it. Now as I had reconciled my beliefs in my initial awakening, I had researched many different religions from my own, by reading the Bible, to Taoism, to Buddhism, and Wicca. I found many parallels between them and many differences. My greatest discovery is that no matter which one I researched, I found common ground, I found oneness. It is our ego that seeks that which divides to make us feel safe, our souls do not. We all peacefully coexist in heaven and this I know because I've channeled people of all beliefs and denominations, sexes, and races. None of it matters. So, when I asked Jesus for guidance regarding my epiphany with the recognition of my inclusivity wound, do you know what he said? "So as you crossed the lines of your fear in seeking love, to discover your oneness with others, now welcome them to cross their lines and fear me not." That small childhood wound was part of a much larger one in the world.

Do you know how many people have been incarnated on this earth at this time that have yet to realize their purpose as dissolving the boundaries to our oneness in love? Many. Part of my soul contract was most assuredly to take a deep dive into the darkness and shadows of my own separateness from self. As I healed my separateness of self, I held space for others to do the same. I stood in my power to take my light into the dark spaces and to alchemize the fear, for I knew and trusted in my ability to do so over and over. So is to become the light to guide others through their own fears. To their own ability to alchemize their own darkness like a chemist into light, for when we do, we alchemize the darkness of the world into more light. It requires great faith and bravery. Spirit tells me many have incarnated to be gay, lesbian, bisexual, transgender, or non-binary in order to dissolve the lines to love. In order to rise above the fear of man and say, no my brothers and sisters these lines were not in fact created by Jesus, they were created by the fears of man. Some of us incarnated as different races and religions with the same message just a different creed. And so, I took that message from Jesus, and I ran with it. My spirit guides had been guiding me for months prior to do a free webinar on reconciling religion. Many of my Christian followers that were awakening were struggling with it. I had put it off and put it off, and then realized that was the time. So, I did, and many felt more at peace. Make no mistake it is not Jesus and God shaming you, it is man. Many people persecute me every day, and tell me I am evil, I am a sinner, I work with the devil and demons, I am a scam artist, and I should be ashamed of myself. It takes every bit of my faith in myself and in Jesus to persevere. Every time I would start to let these things get to me, I would here "Fight Song" by Rachel Patten playing in my head. If you don't know the words, they go something like this, "This is my fight song, take back my life song, prove I'm alright song, my power's turned on, starting right now, I'll be strong, I'll play my fight song, and I don't really care if nobody else believes, 'cause I've still got a lot of fight left in me." Ironically, I would pray and meditate, and it would always be Jesus showing up, grabbing my hand and pulling me back into the spiritual arena to speak my truth. I'm not going to lie, there were many days I questioned the road I was on. Not only that, but seeing mediums like Doreen Virtue, whom I once looked up to completely denounce their work, to call it a lie, made things even more confusing. This is exactly what brought me to learn to not rely on the word as it flows through others, to trust what flows through me. They will have you believing that the difficulty you face in your life is "demonic." I wish I had someone who told me that they had walked through that fire, and tested the waters, and that it was not true, but I didn't. I had to walk through it myself and more than likely you will too.

The seekers and mystics you see turn back to their conventional religion and denounce mysticism as "wrong" are doing so out of fear. There is safety within the confines of what feels known, even if it's not true. I do not shame them for that. What I mean by safety is that it feels safe to our ego. There are no demons, but the ones that exist in your mind. The test is you testing your belief, and your conditioning. You will tremble and shake. I did. I used all sorts of protection rituals until I realized that too was unnecessary. I was still giving away my power to something outside of me. One day spirit gave me the message, "Jules, you are the sage," meaning, my vibration was far more powerful at cleansing my aura and my room than the sage, I just didn't believe it. What I've learned on my journey is we all have light and dark within us. At any moment we choose which is in the driver's seat.

I have learned that the demons we slay are the ones within, that keep us from the truth of who we really are. As long as they exist in the shadows within, the world will be able to poke them and the fear of facing them. It's a journey for the brave. It will test your mental capacity; this is why many turn back and give up. I'm here to say do not. It was beneath the veils of fear that were instilled in me I discovered truth and my power. Once I did, the fear was not there anymore. My clarity to interpret energy skyrocketed. Everywhere I go I see the world misinterpreting energy because they see it through the lens of fear and conditioning. I hope someday that evolves, but the only way it will is for more of us to be brave enough to walk through the fire and rise from the ashes to speak of it. The only monsters that exist are the ones you believe in and give power to. The only monsters that can ever instill fear in me now are the ones with a body. Ya know, the peopley kind. Those are the little buggers you cannot control.

Most of these same people will spout off to me that mediumship is condemned in the Bible. And it is, but in my interpretation, not the mediumship that I practice.

Everything we do comes down to our intention and what we use it for. Many people years ago were charlatans. Not true mediums. They were using mediumship solely for personal gain, or sorcery, not for good. In addition, for anyone who did use it, there was no understanding of it. That kind of power was to be feared. What better way for man to keep man controlled and from becoming more powerful than their leaders? What better way to instill shame and fear for the thought of using such power at all? So, to my critics, I now ask, who wrote the bible? And please recite the verse you speak of with its interpretation. Not one has been able to answer thus far in a decade, without first googling it. They cannot say because all they know is what they heard. They've never done the work. If I told you that elephants were actually eagles, you would question me. So why are we as a collective also not questioning what is perpetuating our wounds through generations and times and stifling our expansion? Those that engage in inquisitive conversation I will ask, did you know Saint Padre Pio was a medium? He channeled the dead and bore the wounds of the stigmata. The Catholic Church kept him hidden for years until they felt he was able to prove his gifts. Then they canonized him a saint. His body, although never embalmed is fully preserved in a glass case in Italy and can be visited to this day. People believe if they touch it, they can still receive his healing energy. I'm thankful for Saint Padre Pio standing in his truth to dispel the fear; he paved a road with his light. I can't help but believe that Padre Pio came here to show us that all who are willing to walk through the fire to truth and be seen will receive some wounds of persecution to do so, but the reward is far greater than you can imagine.

Now I'm not a theologist, but I do also read the Bible and have done some of my own research. Speculation is that the Old Testament was written by Moses and the New Testament was written by the apostles, all prophets, nobody definitively knows. There are 400 years between the writing of these scriptures and yes, they are very different in tone, storyline and messages. If you took the Tao Te Ching, which was written by Lao Tzu, and compared it to the New Testament, you would be astounded at the similarities. The Tao was written hundreds of years before the New Testament! At no point ever is the Bible claimed to be written by Jesus. It is all written by man who was said to be "channeling" the word of God. Yet "channeling" is exactly what modern day man is denounced a sinner for doing. Or is it that just man seeking to stay in power and control of man to prevent man from truly stepping into their power?

You can decide for yourself. Let me share Deuteronomy 18-19 in the Old Testament as a frame of reference for criticism, "When you enter the land the Lord our God is giving you, do not imitate the detestable customs of these nations. No one among you is to sacrifice his son or daughter in the fire, practice divination, tell fortunes, interpret omens, practice sorcery, cast spells, consult a medium or a spiritist, or inquire of the dead. Everyone who does these acts is detestable to the Lord and the Lord your God is driving out the nations before you because of these detestable acts. The Lord you God will raise up for you a prophet like me from among your own brothers, you must listen to him. But the prophet who presumes to speak a message in my name that I have not commanded him to speak, or who speaks in the names of other Gods, that prophet must die. You may say to yourself, how can we recognize a message the Lord has not spoken? When a prophet speaks in the Lord's name and the message does not come true or is not fulfilled that is a message the Lord has not spoken. The prophet has spoken it presumptuously. Do not be afraid of him."

This is the passage that most people criticize mediums for and probably have never even attempted to interpret their own meaning, or meditated about. Do you know what it also says in the Bible? That when the flood came, Noah was 600 years old. That Moses parted the seas. And I could recite the book of Genesis 19-4 which suggests viable and detestable human acts as acceptable, but I won't. Because my goal is not to pull people away from faith or from the Bible or from Jesus. I read scripture. But I use discernment with my interpretation and what I integrate as a belief. Do I believe that Moses parted the seas and that Noah lived to 600 years old? No, I don't. What I will say is this- there are many things in the Bible riddled with fear, judgements, and are aligned with keeping power in the hands of men in power. There are also many things in the Bible that are beautiful life lessons in disguise. I believe that Gospel teachings are meant to be taken metaphorically and applied to one's life in today's times. That is how I use the messages that I channel every day. I let people take them metaphorically and apply them to how they see fit in their own life. Each must decide for themselves what they believe. You can even compare the difference between the old and New Testament. A lot changed in that 400 years. Using a scripture that was written 2000 years ago is like taking a road map from 2000 years ago, walking out onto the street today and expecting it to get you to your destination. How the word flows through you today is what you should believe. I believe as I have channeled with spirit that there will be a new New Testament someday. And I'd be willing to bet a woman will be one of the prophets that channel it. I believe there is a New Testament written each day that we allow God's word to flow through each of us. It is going to take some really strong leadership to dissolve these boundaries as Jesus has supported me in doing and heal the trauma that has been instilled by religious dogma. There is much pain and persecution in this purpose, but there is also great reward in bringing people to Jesus by dissolving the boundaries and the labels we've given one another in fear. So, if your soul needs some scripture to know that Jesus does not support persecuting you for who you are, go to Matthew 5-3 "The Beatitudes" It is my favorite.

"Blessed are the poor in spirit, for the kingdom of heaven is theirs.

Blessed are those who mourn, for they will be comforted.

Blessed are the humble, for they will inherit the earth.

Blessed are those who hunger and thirst for righteousness, for they will be filled.

Blessed are the merciful, for they will be shown mercy.

Blessed are the pure in heart, for they will see God.

Blessed are the peacemakers, for they will be called sons of God.

Blessed are those who are persecuted because of righteousness, for the kingdom of heaven is theirs.

You are blessed when they insult you and persecute you and falsely say every kind of evil against you because of me. Be glad and rejoice because your reward is great in heaven. For that is how they persecuted the prophets who were before you."

There are modern day prophets. I pray to Jesus as we awaken more that community boundaries will love and we will stand up for one another in the true word of God that flows through all of us, love. Let that, your intuition, be your road map, not what any man or woman says that walks beside you, even myself. We all have something we can learn from one another standing in our truth. I'm thankful every day for the persecution that led me to heal my inclusivity wounds to be sovereign enough to speak my voice with confidence. It led me here to speak the truth as I have discovered it and to hopefully give others the courage to walk through the fire of their fears. During your awakening if you feel rejected or persecuted, remember the wise words of Teddy Roosevelt, "It is not the critic who counts; nor, the man who points out how the strong man stumbles, or where the doer of deeds could have done them better. The credit belongs to the man who is actually in the arena, whose face is marred by dust and sweat and blood; who strives valiantly; who errs, who comes short again and again, because there is no effort without error and shortcoming; but who does actually strive to do the deeds; who knows great enthusiasms, the great devotions; who spends himself in a worthy cause; who at best knows in the end the triumph of high achievement, and who at the worst, if he fails, at least fails while daring greatly, so that his place shall never be with those cold and timid souls who neither know victory or defeat." I don't know about you, but I'd rather be the one in the arena. So don't let fear hold you back from exploring, from expanding, and from taking a good look at those wounds, there's freedom at stake.

"She traveled this road as a child, wide eyed and grinning she never tired, but now she won't be coming back with the rest, if these are life lessons, she'll take this test, she needs wide open spaces, room to make her big mistakes, she needs new faces, she knows the higher stakes, she knows the higher stakes." ~Dixie Chicks

JULIE CLAPP

REFLECTIONS & NOTES CHAPTER 14

Chapter 15

"There is no safer space than the one you learn to hold for yourself." ~ Me

October 1st, 2021, I lie in bed awake at 2am and I see a clairvoyant image in my head that says "Exodus 3:14" so clearly. So, I got up to look it up. It is when God came to Moses on the Mount to say, "I am that I am, thus shalt thou say unto the children of Israel, I am hath sent me unto you." I sat contemplating this message. "I am" is God. So, the message here is "I am God, and God sent me to you." This I wholeheartedly believe, and it took a lot of healing work for me to get to that belief and believe it. We are all God. As Rumi said, "You are not a drop in the ocean, you are the ocean in a drop." When I started this journey, my conscious belief was that I was but a glimmer of God expressed on this earth. Now I believe I am the earth, I am God in a glimmer. I am only limited in any moment by that consciousness and perspective of myself in relationship to the world and the universe in which I live and breathe.

I believe that every encounter we have with another human being is of divine orchestration. That does not mean we are not challenged, abused, or hurt by some of those people. That means even those who challenge us, abuse us, or hurt us, will not stop us, because we are the divine. We can use it to disempower us, or we can use it to be a catalyst for something within us to shift or transform. A catalyst to heal, to overcome, to accept, to love, or to end a particular cycle and start anew. When we do the work to see from that perspective, we become grateful for parts of us that are revealed through the toughest experiences of our lives, for without them, we would not have come into the realization of who we are. Ironically two days prior to receiving that message, I had a healing session with an Alchemist named Sandra. Again, I found her through mutual online connections, and I felt spirit guide me to book a session with her and so I did.

At the beginning of the session, we talk about what my intentions are before Sandra starts the healing. She asks me to sink into the most uncomfortable emotion that brought me to her. Oh boy. So, I do, and she tells me she senses my fear. And, in one moment I see I still fear some of my emotions. She asks me to just sit still until I feel it start to dissipate. Yes, I preach stillness and I often practice it, but when I feel uncomfortable emotions, I typically enter into a practice to alleviate them as soon as possible. She was telling me not to. She was telling me I didn't need to immediately reach for higher ground like I'm so used to doing to feel better. So, I sit, and I feel a tingling sensation, almost coolness like menthol or peppermint in my solar plexus chakra right above the belly button. It is responsible for your confidence, self-esteem, and personal power or sovereignty. The uncomfortable emotion is gone. I ask Sandra, "what did you just do to my solar plexus chakra?" She said, "nothing, you did that for yourself." I'm not gonna lie, my initial thought was, "is this the placebo effect, I mean I thought I paid for healing." She said, "I just showed you how to hold space for yourself. She went on to say you need to pretend your emotions are your baby. Babies actually have very few needs, and when they cry, they are simply expressing their needs. So, when your baby cries, hold that baby, comfort that baby, see what it needs and embrace it; don't fear it, it will pass." I was fearing the cries instead of recognizing them as me needing comfort from me. Sandra continued to let me know that essentially my feelings are asking me to "have my own back." To stop denying them, shaming them, fearing them, or trying so vehemently to rise from them. Now it was time to hold them, thank them, comfort them, and validate them because no other can truly do that for us. A new self-reliance was born within me.

Sandra does the healing and then calls me to discuss all the things that my higher-self did for me. She says, "you are learning how to surf your emotions." Now I am astounded because while she was doing the healing, I had a clairvoyant vision of myself surfing! She did not know that because I did not tell her! She said my higher-self activated my sovereignty and inner fortitude, essentially activating a frequency of energy within that says and I quote, "I can surf a tidal wave kind of energy." Another vision I had during the healing was me in a tunnel. I almost felt as though I was in a time warp, which I had never experienced before. Like I was traveling between many lifetimes I had lived. What I was seeing as I traveled through this tunnel was like a cyclone or vacuum of so much light energy coming back to me through my solar plexus chakra. Sandra validates this back to me by telling me my higher-self called back any energy that was unjustly taken from me without my consent, across many lifetimes. Those are sometimes the lessons that we can carry over from previous lives or can come here to try to conquer for our ancestors who weren't able to.

This made me realize that it was even more important for me to stand in my sovereignty. She proceeds to tell me I'm a starseed, and I'm willing to bet if you're still reading this, you are too! Starseed is an old soul with deep inner wisdom and consciousness that incarnates at a certain time to alchemize their own darkness into light, bring forth the knowledge and wisdom gained throughout the process in order to contribute to raising the consciousness and vibration of the earth. Essentially bring in more light. So, if this sounds like you, give yourself some credit. Starseeds are often overachievers, empathic and often feel like they are different or don't belong anywhere. This I have learned is because you came here to get to know you. To feel like you fit with yourself. To center in self. To fit in would require some level of self-abandonment, and that is counterproductive to what your soul came here for. If this rings true for you, rest assured, you've just unlocked a new level of your consciousness that comes with this truth. So congratulations!

JULIE CLAPP

REFLECTIONS & NOTES CHAPTER 15

Chapter 16

"To everything there is a season and a time to every purpose under the heaven." ~The Byrds

When you're neck deep in a healing journey, you are constantly seeking a reprieve from the density. If you've done this work before you know what I mean. It is cycles of feeling deep emotions, processing them, rising, rinsing, and then seemingly repeating. Ironically during this time, my mom fell ill with shingles. I had a family trip planned and I knew we just wouldn't be able to go. My other sisters stepped in and offered to take turns staying and caring for my mom so that we could go. I had been back and forth to the emergency room with her a few times because she had shown symptoms of TIA or mini strokes. Her CT scans were negative and both times they sent her home. I had gotten her a home cardiac monitor just to be safe. I was exhausted. I hadn't been sleeping because I was sleeping on my mom's couch in case she needed me in the middle of the night. The break to Florida was much needed. When I got there, I slept the whole first day and through the night. I was worried about my mom, but I felt comfortable with her in the hands of my sisters. When we returned, she was much the same as when I had left so I decided to still stay with her. I cleared most of my schedule to keep an eye on her and take her to her follow up appointments. One morning she woke up and she could not form her words. I called 911 and they took her back to the hospital to be reevaluated for a stroke. They felt as though she was having mini strokes and wanted to put her on an additional blood thinner. My mom was already taking aspirin, but she was terrified of taking blood thinners. She had a bad experience in the past with them. They tried to convince her that this was a different one she could try and necessary to prevent her from having a stroke. She reluctantly agreed and we took her home. It took months for her to recover, and she still had some lasting effects. Over the course of those few months, I noticed that my response to stress was not my typical anxiety. It wasn't just panic attacks. I was experiencing far more symptoms of my nervous system despite all the healing I had been doing. It felt disheartening. I was starting to lose my faith. My mom is stoic and clear at what she wants and doesn't want. As a nurse it is hard to convince someone to do what you think is best for their wellbeing when they don't want it. This triggered me back into wanting to fix or control in order to make myself feel better. After all, I wasn't sleeping, I wasn't able to work, and I wasn't able to fix the situation. This time the feeling of having no control over a situation that very much impacted my life was manifesting much louder in my physical body. All of my bells and whistles were sounding. Over the course of the next few months, I kept using all my tools, but they weren't enough. I decided to revisit the idea of cognitive behavioral therapy. I went on the website and read the bios of the practitioners. One stood out to me that I hadn't seen before. Something in my gut said try her. So I did and she happened to be taking new patients. Enter Kelly.

It felt like as I started to describe how I was feeling, she already knew the answer. She validated how I was feeling and asked some questions so that she could give me some things to reflect on. She validated the same information that I had received pretty much from every other healer I had seen, but from a psychological standpoint, not an energy standpoint. She said that more than likely a lot of my nervous system dysregulation and anxiety stemmed from self-abandonment, people pleasing and co-dependency. One of the biggest gifts she gave to me was the book, "Codependent No More." As I read the pages I thought, "this is me." I was able to learn about relationship attachment styles. I could see more clearly how I attached to certain people and how others were attached to me. Anxious attachers usually are anxious, overread situations, overthink outcomes, and seek a lot of validation from people in their life to feel safe and secure in the bond. The goal for me was to become a secure attacher. That started with the relationships I felt most safe in, and the ones that mirrored secure attachment back to me. This was a critical part of my journey because I realized in the process of manifestations, if we have anxious attachment in relationships, we don't feel safe and worthy of love as we are. This will carry over into feeling worthy and safe to receive other things that are on the same frequency of love, like abundance, and freedom. I couldn't help but think this was another stepping stone to raising my frequency. The hardest part of my awakening has been the realization that I developed patterns of behavior to make myself feel safe, worthy, and loved, and they did the exact opposite. Codependency is basically emotional enmeshment with the people you love and care about. It leads to emotional dysregulation for many reasons. First you are putting the needs of others before your own. Second, you lack strong enough boundaries to self-preserve and declare how you deserve or need to be treated and loved not just to survive, but to thrive. Third, you will tell yourself you can only be ok if everyone you care about is ok first. And lastly, all of these things will cause you to be hypervigilant and hyper-attuned to your environment as a protective mechanism of, you guessed it, the amygdala. As we stated before that is the part of your brain that is responsible for your survival techniques. My survival techniques screamed self-abandonment for far too long. And even though I had been doing better with my people pleasing, I was unaware of how much codependency in my relationships was impacting me. I had told myself that getting better at saying "No" was the answer. And while that was part of it, it wasn't the core. Kelly was showing me the core. I didn't like to set boundaries with people I love because I viewed it as selfish. I felt guilty distancing from people that were not treating me the way I deserved being treated. I tolerated behaviors that were in fact harming me, but I was in denial of it. I would rather cause myself discomfort than be the cause of another's discomfort. I would rather stay in a relationship that didn't serve me, to avoid guilt and grieving a relationship with someone I deeply cared for. I would hold on to the potential or the illusion of what I thought the relationship could be, versus what the experience of it actually was. My inner child was screaming through my nervous system once again that I needed to have her back.

The symptoms I was experiencing felt like I had PTSD. Seemingly simple things that I could've easily handled before could trigger a tsunami in my nervous system. I researched and discussed CPTSD with Kelly. If you've never heard of CPTSD, my understanding is that it is similar symptoms to PTSD, but not necessarily from one traumatic event. It can occur from a series of small traumas that seemingly fly under the radar for a period of years and can stem from narcissistic abuse. Now I know the words narcissism and gaslighting are becoming overused buzzwords in society, but I truly believe it is because for so long, it went unrecognized, especially by those on the receiving end. More people are talking about it now, so there is more awareness. I did learn in therapy that there is a wide array of narcissism, it is not one size fits all. There is actually a criteria that needs to be met for a true diagnosis of narcissistic personality disorder. What many describe as narcissism can actually just be similar behaviors or traits from another cause. I find that many empaths on a spiritual awakening journey have suffered some narcissistic injury in their lifetime and are also at risk for developing controlling or narcissistic tendencies as a result. I believe this is more than likely because we are so empathic and have difficulty setting boundaries, which are the perfect keys for the narcissistic lock or trauma bond because those are the very qualities that make us manipulatable. Plus, we like to see the best in others. But over time, narcissistic abuse and gaslighting will also contribute to nervous system dysregulation. If anything, the thing I learned about narcissism that stuck with me is there too seems to be deep unhealed trauma and worthiness wounds at the core. Ironically, many of the behaviors also seem to be subconscious patterns of the ego to feel safe, in control, and loved. Because of my belief in mirroring and projecting, I can't tell you how many times I asked my therapist, are you sure I'm not doing this? The key component she would often reflect back to me is that narcissism typically lacks self-reflection and accountability because of the fragility of the wounded ego. The intrinsic need of the narcissist to hold on to their false perception of self will supersede any need of anyone outside of them. It feels that threatening. I feel this is why there is an inability for narcissists to truly empathize with others and in any given situation will take on the role of the victim.

The other thing I recognized was that because I had a dominant belief that nervous system triggers reveal something to be healed, me being triggered felt like I was never doing enough to heal. She said, "or you keep throwing yourself back into the environment that's hurting you. It's like trying to put a fire out when someone is fanning the flames." So, triggers are not just a sign of a need for healing. They are your nervous system letting you know when there is something harmful happening to you that you may or may not be consciously aware of, which is often the case with gaslighting or manipulating behavior. Sometimes it takes a long time to see it and even longer to accept it. During that process of grieving the illusion of what we thought was, these triggers will feel even stronger. Once you become aware of them, your nervous system will sound the alarms louder to protect you and prevent further injury. This is why retreating into the self, like a turtle retreating into the safety of its shell is so therapeutic in healing. This grieving process is often the discomfort we like to avoid, Kelly calls it "bargaining" and apparently, I love to bargain.

As I would fight for bargaining, I would revisit some of my old patterns that felt safe. I learned to be gentle with myself when I did instead of always beating myself up. I realized the list of roles my ego had taken on was growing in my awareness. And the only way to end those roles was to start loving all of those parts of me that were trying to protect me and to let little Jules know, that I knew how to protect us now. See if any of these roles resonate with you.

The Perfectionist: if everything in my environment and my life is just so, I feel ok, but when it is not, I don't, I feel out of control.

The People Pleaser: It's just easier to do what they want me to do instead of dealing with it. I.e., I don't want to feel the discomfort of their disappointment with me.

The Martyr: I have to do everything myself, if I don't do it, it won't get done right anyway so I might as well just do it.

The Fixer: Once I fix everything and create external peace, I will allow myself to have internal peace.

I realized with Kelly that some of these patterns can become addictive. Meaning we become so conditioned to these survival techniques our brain actually provides us with hits of dopamine and serotonin from the contentment of continuing them. Studies show that many people that have these survival techniques for long periods of time actually have enlarged amygdalas. I felt like I had been baking a pie for the last three years, and that Kelly had just given me the missing ingredients to complete it. I knew this was going to be a lifelong thing for me. There were no more quick fixes. I mean don't get me wrong, it felt somewhat comforting to know that there was a psychological explanation to what I was experiencing, but I knew I had to change it. I mean after all, placing blame on my overactive amygdala wasn't going to get me far. I didn't want to survive anymore, I wanted to thrive. She would often remind me that healing was not a destination. This helped me to stay present with whatever I felt each day instead of looking too far ahead and placing expectations on what this leg of the journey would look like. It was important for me once again to define my edges, to acknowledge that I had needs and to start to put those needs first. To honor the little girl in me who had birthed a belief that enlightenment, compassion and love meant giving to everyone else but herself. The truth was the little girl in me did not feel safe.

Over the next six months I started to notice my hormones shifting as many women my age do. My doctors assured me my levels were fine but that I could be experiencing some symptoms of perimenopause. I started to get UTI's more frequently. I had two of them back-to-back. I had lots of bloating, pelvic pain, bladder pain and overall discomfort. I had symptoms of what felt like neuropathy extending down my legs into my feet. I was holding on to excess weight around my abdomen because of my stress hormones, and because of my discomfort I was also unable to exercise in the ways I normally would. A part of me also believes that empaths will sometimes subconsciously hold on to a bit of extra weight around the midsection where their solar plexus chakra is as a means of protection. It's like a shield to cushion the blows. As an energy person I have always needed to move my body. It is critical for my mental, physical, and energetic health. So, I would make sure I would walk every day at least a mile during this time. I couldn't understand why at this part in my healing journey, when I was finally starting to see things so clearly mentally, my physical health seemed to be falling apart. Over the next few months, I went through testing and saw different doctors. Nothing showed up. I started to do online research and I found so many women with the same thing. I decided to take matters into my own hands and try a holistic approach. I started urinary supplements and probiotics that encouraged flushing the biofilm in the bladder and relaxing the bladder muscles to prevent spasms. One of the doctors I had seen also encouraged pelvic floor exercises to strengthen my pelvic floor muscles which can weaken as we age and estrogen levels lower. In addition, during this time I committed to meditating and journaling or automatic writing every day. Because I had spent so much time in fight or flight where the nervous system produces too much of our stress hormones, adrenaline, and cortisol, I realized the importance of stimulating my parasympathetic nervous system, which tells the body it's ok to "rest and digest." I started doing diaphragmatic breathing exercises to stimulate the vagus nerve, the largest nerve in the body. I started using tapping, aka EFT, "Emotional Freedom Technique" as a tool to deescalate dense emotions and alleviate stress hormones when I would feel them.

One day when I was meditating for guidance about my pelvic symptoms a distinct memory came up for me. When I was four years old, I suffered UTI's. I had ureteral valve reflux which caused urine to back up into my kidneys. It required tests where they would irrigate my bladder with a catheter under ultrasound to see if the valve was working properly. I also had to undergo surgery, after which they gave me too much pain medicine. It caused a paralytic ileus where my bowels stopped moving and it required them to put a tube down my nose and into my stomach to decompress it. Because of the extent of the surgery, I had lost a lot of blood and that required a blood transfusion. I have vivid memories of all of this. What came up for me in my meditations is that I had energetically stored a lot of trauma in this area of my body. A part of my anxiety was manifesting in my pelvis because that is where the root and sacral chakras or energy centers are and that is where we hold our sense of safety and security. In all of my 46 years, I never even realized I had any trauma. If I told you my experiences even though they were scary obviously being a kid, they were not what I would have called "bad." My Mom took me to the best of the best doctors and surgeons. She stayed by my side the whole time, always advocating for me. But I realize now, especially being a nurse, is that when we do medical procedures it can be difficult, especially with children to cultivate a feeling of safety and security during some of them. The truth is the procedures I had required me to lie on a table, no clothes, my legs open, and a catheter inserted inside of me. You can explain that to the cows come home to a four-year-old and I can tell you, there will more than likely still be some trauma stored from that experience. Even if it remains hidden in the shadows.

I had stored trauma in my nervous system and in my pelvis for 40 years and I didn't even know it until it physically manifested. The more I did exercises that released trauma the better I started to feel. I also did a lot of inner child work. So, when I would feel stressed, I would comfort and soothe my inner child. I know it sounds simple, but you would be amazed how this technique alleviates nervous system stress hormone release. I continued the practice of strengthening and relaxing my pelvic floor muscles and my neuropathic and pelvic pain started to feel a lot better. Now I'm completely back to myself and I have found a new passion for Pilates. I did go back to taking Citalopram also because I was focused on regulating my nervous system and I knew it could only help. Again, it proved to be a miracle for me. I couldn't help but smirk at the fact that what was healing me the most was actually a combination of both eastern and western medicine. But ultimately it was my intuition that guided me to each practitioner, to all of my research, books, and ultimately to my healing.

REFLECTIONS & NOTES CHAPTER 16

Chapter 17

"This is Me"

"When the sharpest words want to cut me down, I'm gonna send a flood, gonna drown them out, I am brave, I am bruised, I am who I'm meant to be, this is me. Look out cause here I come, And I'm marching on to the beat I drum, I'm not scared to be seen, I make no apologies, this is me." ~Keala Settle

---

Part of awakening the parts of yourself that heal, alchemize, and align you, means letting go of the old parts of you. I remember lying in bed with my husband one night and I said, "Am I different? Like am I the same girl you married all those years ago, when I was a nurse?" He said, "you're the same, you've always been this way." By this way he means curious and stubborn about exploring whatever I'm curious about in that moment. This gave me immediate relief, which I know was my ego needing to be validated, but it felt good in that moment. Sometimes when you feel yourself going through a growth spurt, you almost don't recognize your new self because you've shed so many illusions that your old self carried around. You view and experience the world completely differently. That can be a lonely place if the people you are closest to you don't have the same view. It can cause distance and resistance energetically because your beliefs might not align anymore and so your everyday choices, conversations, actions, and behaviors may also not align. Many will resist the new parts of you. We like one another to be predictable because predictability feels safe. That is why people come to me for readings. The truth is, we are most certainly always going to be unpredictable beings because we are ever-evolving beings. We aren't static; we don't stand still. Part of my awakening was allowing the evolution of my soul and coming into full acceptance of my new consciousness. The more I sought validation without, the more I would feel like I didn't fit in, the more I would stifle my own growth or shrink myself back into the old me. Trust me that is even more uncomfortable in the long haul. Eventually, the more self-love and self-acceptance I gave to the process of my evolution, the more I allowed my seasons to change and the more I accelerated my growth. Everyone is on their own journey of consciousness. We don't get to decide where anyone else is presently or when and how they evolve. As you heal, you evolve, your vibration changes and your alignment changes. Everything changes to match your new frequency. So inevitably there will be distance created with whatever you previously aligned with in your old frequency. That will be everything from the food you eat to the work you do, to the people you feel most yourself around. These are how your seasons are defined.

Inherently we are conditioned to believe that distance or resistance is bad, and so suffering ensues. It's actually the opposite, distance and resistance are signs of growth and listening to inner guidance. If you acknowledge resistance, you are being asked to pause and maneuver something or someone who may be an obstacle to your growth at that leg of your journey. I remember someone asking me one day, "so do you think we just have seasons with one another, and that's it?". There was a grief-like sadness in the tone. I didn't answer the question because I knew life would eventually answer that question, but in my head I thought, "yes, that is it, and that is ok." I also had awareness that I was at a different place where my consciousness no longer feared those changes in my seasons. We cannot control who chooses to grow with us and we cannot stifle our growth for those who choose not to; both cause suffering. We have seasons where we grow, we shift, we integrate at a new frequency, and we align with new people, places, and experiences. We grieve what we leave behind and what sometimes leaves us behind. Do you live at home with your parents forever? Do you skip going off to college or taking trips, or getting your own home? Why not? Because innately we know that depth of love is not defined by the extent with which we will stifle our growth. Love is allowing growth. Love is supporting growth. It takes nothing from you, it expands you. In that same scenario is it not painful and scary for the child going off to college and is it not painful and scary for the parents? Of course it is, but we do it anyway. Mostly because society has told us that is ok. Society has yet to catch up with the evolution of the soul and get the word out, that all seasons are ok. Actually, I've had people in my life that were a great part of one season, then were distant for a period of time only to miraculously align again with me later on. As if the universe had conspired to make it happen. I believe wholeheartedly that only happened because both myself, and the other people were in a complete state of acceptance and allowance of what was at each moment. We were surrendered to the flow of the universe.

So you see, love defies space and time. That's why I can communicate with your loved ones in heaven. The love is the frequency of that station. The vibration is the song, the language between us. I'm the medium, I'm just the receiver of the song. You can honor seasons and even when they change, grieve them, but try not to shame or blame them. As much as I've repeated these cycles of healing over the years, there is always a part of the cycle where the gratitude is immense. Let me be clear, not for the traumas, not for the way things may have unfolded. I have no intent to sensationalize trauma. I feel grateful for what I received, what I got, what I now know that I didn't before. I feel grateful for becoming more of me. Cue Snoop Dog, "I wanna thank me." These seasons are the fingerprint, the lasting impression on your soul, the core memories. Even when they end, they go with you, they become you. The only thing that tells you otherwise is your ego wanting to shrink you back into what you've known and what feels comfortable or relatable to society. The demands of the society we live in will tell you, you "should" be doing something other than what you are. To be honest, some of the people nearest and dearest to my heart I have gone months, even years without seeing or talking to and when we do align, there is no awkwardness. In fact, there is excitement and anticipation to catch up and celebrate who we are now.

Most of the people closest to me know I am not one to text, call, or reach out often. I am not a slave to my phone, and I have learned that I do not need to be emotionally available to anyone other than myself and my children 24/7. The people that love me, accept that about me and don't take it personally. If this is something you tend to take personally with people in your life, you have to start asking yourself, what is the part of you that feels insecure in your relationship? What other people do or don't do, has all to do with them. What you do or don't do, has all to do with you. This life is me against me and you against you, not me against you. That is our oneness. My brother-in-law said to me one day when I was probably babbling about one of my theories, "ya know people don't think about you as much as you think, they are too busy thinking about themselves." Ain't that the truth and so they should be focused on their own journey, and so should we. When we each focus on both of those things, when we do come together, we can truly celebrate one another. We need to give one another the permission to stop trying to force square pegs into round holes; it's causing great suffering. As you lean into acceptance, much of that suffering ends.

Nobody gets to define what is best for you, and you don't get to define what is best for someone else. You will align when you align, you won't when you don't. Forcing only causes more friction not love. I am also a firm believer in face-time with people. It is easy to take things personally when you are distant for long periods and not sharing space with another. When you are in the presence of someone, you can feel their energy much more than you will feel their words. That is what matters, how you feel in the presence of the energy. That cues you in if you are aligning or if you are not. Either is ok! Neither is bad! No-one is better than the other! They are just at two different points on a map at that moment. Like poet Billy Chapata says, "don't measure the strength of your connections off of what people can do for you, measure them off which connections allow you to stay most connected to yourself."

REFLECTIONS & NOTES CHAPTER 17

Chapter 18

"You're gonna hear me roar." ~Katie Perry

I remember telling each of the healers I worked with that I felt as though some of the trauma I was healing was either stemming from a past life or from my ancestors. Many of us have soul contracts that are fulfilled by our healing. As we heal ourselves, we heal our lineage from the past and for the future. It is no easy task and innately you may feel this. I had many visions of previous lives where my intuitive and healing abilities were not only dishonored, but they were also shamed in public and exploited for personal gain in private. So, in this lifetime I know my soul came to take back my power and energy and stand in the sovereignty of my abilities. In order for me to fully come into my power, I had to learn to rise from complete disempowerment. As I learned more of the truth of who I am, I birthed an inner confidence and sense of self. My strong sense of self and wellbeing only enhanced my spiritual abilities. It helped me to clearly "know" and trust my energy so that I can readily define, interpret, and maneuver energy outside of me without letting it consume me. My ability to read the room fine-tuned like a navigation system. The once edge of my sword that kept getting me caught up, now became the edge that glided me through the density of this earth. My ability to define the edges of where I ended in a room of many energies became stronger than ever, without anyone else but myself even knowing. As a result of creating this newfound safety within my energy field and my physical body, my anxiety healed greatly. I will never say that I have fully "healed" my anxiety or depression or any other emotion we've come as a society to label as "bad." I feel these are normal human emotions that we are meant to feel in all of their intensity at times and to let them reveal something to us that was behind a veil of our consciousness. Because I no longer suffer from anxiety every day, I am now able to view it as just a way my body is communicating a need or a guidance to me in any given moment. There are no "bad" emotions in my mind anymore and that greatly lessens my fear of feeling them. They all play a great role in meeting our needs. Imagine if we had been taught that right from the get-go?

Empaths are often anxious because they are constantly interpreting an overwhelming amount of energy and stimuli like a sponge, soaking it in without realizing it.

Without a strong sense of self-awareness, we lose our edge, we don't have boundaries, and we become enmeshed with energy outside of ourselves. This makes us feel anxious, and erodes our self-trust and intuitive voice for ourselves. Grounding exercises were pivotal for me in helping my anxiety. We can do this through daily envisionment techniques of literally grounding our physical body to the earth. We can also sit and press our sitz bones at the base of the spine on a hard surface like a wooden chair or floor. Redirecting much of our energy that is utilized in our upper energy centers down to our lower energy centers is very grounding.

Empaths, intuitives, and healers spend a lot of time giving attention to their intuitive centers, which is your third eye chakra in the middle of your forehead, and your crown chakra on the top of your head. In addition, your communication center is in your throat and your heart chakra is in your chest. The energy centers that ground you are your root chakra at the base of your spine, which is responsible for your sense of safety and security, and your solar plexus chakra above your belly button which is responsible for your self-esteem and empowerment. I gave a lot of attention to these lower energy centers when I was healing to help me cultivate self-trust, safety and security within. I've included a link to a free meditation I recorded called, "safety and security" if you feel as though you need help with this. In addition, when you get outside and connect with the frequency of nature, it is naturally grounding. It pulls your energy down toward the ground as it raises your vibration to match the frequency of the earth. Have you ever noticed how peaceful you feel by water? That is because energetically water is a natural cleanser and purifier to our aura or energy field to rid of us any accumulated or stuck energy. The aura is a buffer zone. It's this invisible field around us where outside energy impresses upon us. I say when spirit is connecting with me, I can feel them impressing on my aura as if they are knocking on my door and asking if it's ok to come in. I mostly say yes, except at 3am! I will politely ask them to come back later. When I go out in nature, I often would envision all the trees as energy sources, full of bright white light. I would envision pulling that light into my solar plexus energy center and letting it rise within me, filling up my entire body. Then I would let this light turn into golden honey and as it poured out of me, encased me in its purity, providing a barrier for my energy field. It's another way to draw energy back into your solar plexus when you feel as though you may be leaking energy out into the world or people around you and unknowingly disempowering yourself. This can happen especially in high stress environments or environments with people that make you feel drained.

Once you come into a stronger sense of yourself, you call back a lot of your energy to empower all of your senses and abilities. Your healing cycles will directly correlate to the leveling up of your other abilities, like your intuition and manifesting. It's a part of the journey that most people in the manifestation community don't readily talk about because manifestation is often painted as "all positivity." The truth that I've learned is that healing ourselves is what heals the vibration in order to manifest at higher frequencies. As we know, healing is not all positive. There is a lot of darkness and depth of emotion. Just know that new depth you travel to, will reveal a new height to you! So, in fact, Joseph Campbell may have actually been right when he said that every feeling fully felt could actually be bliss.

One of the greatest things that has happened as a result of my healing journey is that I take things less personally. I don't mean that I don't feel all those emotions I've previously discussed, but I have a different perspective on them now and I process them much differently than I ever did before. I don't readily accept things at face value. I very much rely on my 6th senses to interpret and navigate the world that I live in. I feel the authenticity in someone's energy far quicker than I trust their words or actions. Because we all say stupid things at times, and we all do things that will inevitably hurt others at times. So sometimes those things don't align with our intentions and can be interpreted as hurtful. What I trust is the energy when words and actions align. That means there is no gap in self at that moment and that is what we call authenticity. And even if there is a gap and I know someone is not being authentic, I don't shame them for that, but would I trust them with my vulnerability? No. Would I consider them a safe space? Also no. The more authentic you become and the safer you feel to express that out into the world, the more you will align with others who live the same way. It is vibrational law. Like attracts like energy. When people come into your experience that you don't line up with, it is so that one of you can mirror something to the other. So, allow your healing to be a mirror of healing and authenticity to the world. Hold gentle space for others to join you there by not shaming, but using boundaries and setting standards for how you will be treated.

Boundaries are a loving way of telling someone you want them in your life, but these are your terms to keep the relationship healthy for you. The more you get comfortable with this and the process of self-reflection, the more clarity you receive in all moments. You will no longer be manipulatable. Trust me when I say, your nervous system and your intuition will smell it from a mile away. But the beautiful part is that you will no longer be reactionary because you've tended your emotional state of being. You know how to soothe you. Your internal climate is no longer dependent on outside circumstances. You go with the flow. And during the times things don't seem to be flowing, you will intuitively reflect on that resistance, knowing that you are being slowed for a purpose or need to be met. Things in life may happen that are beyond our control, but God and the universe is always truly working in our favor to help us through them and to continue to live a beautiful life. Spirit tells me as long as we are in these bodies, we are meant to be giving and receiving love. It's like oxygen for our soul. That exchange can only happen with an open heart. So, on your darkest days, when you want to give up and give in to the darkness, don't. Remind yourself of how amazing you are. You are not a work in progress, you are perfect always just as you are in God's eyes. There is no need to beat yourself or others up, when you do, you only instill more shame to be healed. Space and time create a gap for love, self-love. And self-love as I know it is the greatest transformer of all time.

When you feel scared, hold your inner child. When you feel weak, reach for something to hold you up. When you feel sad, soothe the part of you that is missing love. When you feel angry, dance in it. Anger is such a beautiful and undervalued part of the healing process. Let the rage move through you. Allow yourself to get dark. I called it getting in touch with my inner witch. I was always afraid to admit as a Catholic that I thought I may have been a witch in a previous life, but a good witch, like Glinda in the "Wizard of Oz." Nobody thought witches were good back then. When you shine a light on her, the girl who was afraid to feel rage and anger for fear it would define her, you allow her to emerge with a capacity for love like you've never known. Trust me I've done it. I kept her hidden in the shadows of shame for most of my life. She has permission to be seen, and so now, anger has no hold on me. It flows like a river through me, always leading me to new shores. When you feel jealous, I want you to remind yourself of something, there is something you desire that you feel like is not yet in your possession. You attracted that person to show you that it is possible for you. It is a sign that you have deep desire being birthed within you and to go for it. Stop waiting.

When you feel joy and gratitude and bliss, you know all the emotions we label as the "good guys," feel them fully. Let them course and pulse through your body enough to raise your arms in the air and bring tears through your eyes. That is what you came for. You travel through darkness and climb mountains for those moments whether you realize it or not. For God sakes, feel them and milk them and make it your dominant intent to make them contagious. And when you feel tired, remember these things. Healing the nervous system decreases the level of stress hormones that have been your fuel for years. As those levels of cortisol lower, you will be tired. You will feel unmotivated. This is where you take out the soft blanket, you light the candle, you pour the cup of tea, you put on your most favorite feel-good movie, and you love on yourself more. Please don't shame your amazing body that is working so hard for you. What a miracle that our hearts beat 100,000 times a day without us even having to give it a single thought! Imagine how long it was beating faster from all that cortisol. It's ok to rest. Your nervous system just went through a war, or so it thinks it did. Be kind to yourself.

I wish I could tell you how beautiful your mind, body and spirit are when they work in synchronicity with one another and you would just believe it, but I know it's not that simple. As you go on this journey, remember I said that. There will come a day when you look back and tears will fill your eyes. You will know you are exactly where you are meant to be, and the contents of your heart will be spilling out pure love. It won't stay that way, it will ebb and flow, but you will feel that like never before. As I closed out this chapter, I felt that. I was sitting on my bed typing and I looked in the corner of my bedroom and saw my grandparents. My mom's mom whom I had never met had tears in her eyes and in her Irish brogue she said to me, "Thank you." There were no words needed for I knew what she was saying. The same thing so many spirits have come through to say to their loved ones, "you helped me to heal." See they didn't get the opportunity to live in a time like we do. They were told not to feel, to be stoic, and to keep their wounds hidden in the secrets and shadows. I knew my nana felt freedom from the work I had done on this earth. I knew some of that pain I felt on my darkest days was in fact hers. I gave a voice to her wounds, I released her rage, and I did things she never had the opportunity to do. Next to her was my grandfather. I have no memory of him; I was four years old when he passed. But my mom shares stories of him. He smiled at me and said, "I couldn't have done it better myself kid." My mom told me my grandfather loved to write. He wrote letters all the time. So did I, since I was a kid, it has been a way for me to express myself that always felt safe. Years ago, my sister did a reiki session on me, and she told me he came through and made it known he was around me. I know why now. It always surprised my mom to know when I would see them, they were together in heaven. They had their fair share of difficulties. But they are, which is such a profound example of the level of love and forgiveness we are capable of here on this earth and in heaven. Anything is possible when we are willing to seek it and believe it.

On the days that you might not believe in yourself, please know I believe enough for both of us now, and so you will never be alone. There is a sacred warrior that is within you that has been calling you through your suffering for years. Notice her. Call on her. Let her be seen and heard. You will astound yourself. As you breathe life back into you with your creator, you breathe life back into your hopes, your dreams and your deepest desires coming to fruition. Franklin Roosevelt said, "Calm seas never made a skilled sailor." What I've learned is that the fool's journey is spending all of your energy trying to control the sea. Calm seas start within the skill of the sailor. Every day that sea tried to get the best of me while I was healing, I would go in my basement and look at a photo of my dad. It was a photo my brother gave me of him sitting on the front of his boat in the sun, on the ocean giving a thumbs up. Every time I would look at it, I would here him, "You got this Jul." I allowed this journey to be guided by both of my fathers in heaven and I honor them by wearing symbols of them on my neck every day. I have a heart from my dad in which he engraved, "small in size, big in life." I hope I'm making him proud by sharing my "big" with you to help you heal.

We may be a drop in the ocean but I know we can each make big waves if we try. With the heart I wear a cross. For Jesus. I almost gave up many times and Jesus was truly my savior that kept me going. That cross reminds me that some of the greatest healing comes through pain and persecution. When I'm hurt, I hear the words, "forgive them for they know not what they do." And it's true. Most of us know not what we do, but that doesn't make it ok. And we can change that. And that change will always start with healing ourselves. It is our best chance at making an impact on this earth.

Finally, I would like you to know that on your darkest days, the ones when you may question why you're here, or how you will get through, there is a hand for you to hold, even when you cannot see it. It is the hand of God. It lies in your hands. And that hand, is more powerful than anything outside of you or any "hand" you may have been dealt. You're beautiful and amazing and you are needed in this world. So please always keep going.

With love and deepest gratitude,

Xo Jules

REFLECTIONS & NOTES CHAPTER 18

JULIE CLAPP

ACKNOWLEDGEMENTS AND
DEDICATION

I would be remiss if I did not acknowledge the people in my life that were my safe spaces. I am awe-inspired by your capacity. You kept me on this earth when I questioned being here, you even got me to laugh, a lot. To my husband Derek, and my two son's Jared and Dylan. You've been my greatest teachers, mirrors, and loving supporters on this journey. I'd walk through any fire for you. You are my heaven on earth and your love breathes life into my soul every day, but especially on my toughest days. I heal for you. You've shown me love that is other worldly! To my family and friends I extend much gratitude for each of you. You truly have brought me to this place of wholeness within and that is the deepest expression of love we can give one another on this earth.

GETTING PRESENT ACTIVITY

Take a deep cleansing breath into the count of three and exhale to the count of six.

Repeat 3 times.

Look around the room and find something soft. Touch it as a reminder there are things that are gentle and soft in this world for you.

Look around the room and find something green, let this serve as a reminder it is safe to keep your heart open.

Look around the room and find something that makes you smile. Remind yourself there is a lot that will make you smile moving forward.

Hold your left hand to your heart. Your left side is your divine feminine energy. It is also your receiver when it comes to manifestation. Take a deep cleansing breath in and recite. I am safe to receive all the love and abundance the universe has to offer me, and so it is.

FREE MEDITATIONS:

Safety & Security Meditation:
https://youtu.be/33Mo6qpQw3s

Ascension 2.0 Meditation (Inner Child healing):
https://youtu.be/VNGL9WQNgYo

Inner Child Healing:
https://youtu.be/ltGR1Y6fz04

BOOKS I RECOMMEND:

Radical Awakening by Dr. Shefali

Claim My Power by Mastin Kipp

The Body Keeps Score by Dr. Bessel van Der Kolk

Codependent No More by Melody Beattie

The Gifts Beneath My Anxiety by Pat Longo

Becoming Supernatural by Dr. Joe Dispenza